D0323851

# Conquer Fear!

*Lisa Jimenez, M.Ed*

Published by
Rx Success, Inc.
4630 N. University Drive
Suite #449
Coral Springs, FL 33067
(954) 755-3670
(800) 489-7391
www.Rx-Success.com

© MMIII by Lisa Jimenez
All Rights Reserved

No part of this book may be reproduced, stored in or introduced
into a retrieval system, or transmitted, in any form or by any means
(electronic, mechanical, photocopying, recording or otherwise)
without the prior written permission of the copyright owner.

ISBN: 0-9705807-0-352700

Manufactured in the United States
10 9 8 7 6 5 4 3 2

Editor: Vicki McCown

# *What people are saying about Conquer Fear!*

"Lisa Jimenez deserves a medal for writing this book. It will free millions of people from a self imposed prison. If you want to multiply your income and begin enjoying a dimension of joy you might not even be able to imagine... devour this magnificent book. I have ordered the first hundred off the press for my loved ones.

—Bob Proctor, Author of *You Were Born Rich*,
Chairman of LifeSuccess Productions

"Lisa takes you through an introspection to overcome the very thing that keeps you from enjoying the blessings of your God-given talents. The chapter on faith helped me accomplish my goals as a Tupperware Manager. Learn to overcome your fears through some very practical steps in Lisa's latest book, Conquer Fear!".

—Pam Burks-Losey, Tupperware Manager

"This is an outstanding book to help you be more, do more, and have more. Overcome your fear and welcome achievement, happiness, and fulfillment with Lisa's book. Read. Benefit. Enjoy."

—Nido R. Qubein, Chairman Creative Services, Inc.

"Is there a person alive who has no fear to conquer? Jimenez has helpful insights on a timely topic in this E-commerce age, when every day presents a changing challenge."

—Dianna Booher, Author of
*Communicate with Confidence, E-Writing, and Well Connected*

"It doesn't matter how smart you are, how many degrees you have, or how much money you make. We all have fears that are holding us back. Lisa's book Conquer Fear is you breakthrough to finally conquering all your fears."

—Juanell Teague, President of People Plus

"Don't let fear keep you from living life to the fullest! Read this book and get the insights that will help you triumph over one of your greatest enemies."

—Mark Sanborn, CSP, CPAE, Sanborn & Associates, Inc.

"I have lived what Lisa writes so I know if you follow her precepts, encouragements and wisdom, you, too, will surprise yourself! When you read this book you will combine faith with courage to make friends with your fear and live an enhanced life."

—Rosita Perez CSP, CPAE, Creative Living Programs, Inc.

"We all have fears that are holding us back. Lisa's book Conquer Fear is your breakthrough to finally conquering all your fears."

—Daryl Gardener, Miami Dolphins

"Lisa's book is liberating! When you're ready to face your fears and shatter the beliefs that hold you back, read this book."

—Tarnesia Gardener, Wife and Mother

"I highly recommend reading "Conquer Fear!". By adopting the principles and practices in this book you can begin to change your life for the better. Lisa clearly illustrates how a life grounded in faith and focused on God is one that will provide the rewards and riches that He has in store for each of us."

—Michael Going, SVP, ANC Rental Corporation,
(President, Alamo Rental)

"Lasting motivation must come from within and is the result of cultivation a positive belief system. Lisa deals with in her book, and showed our sales force how to understand and change a self-defeating set of beliefs into a confident state of mind. I am sure this book "Conquer Fear!" will be the positive reinforcement to the lessons our staff learned through her seminars with them."

—Gary Peters, President La Sal National Bank

"This book should be required reading for everyone in direct sales. Lisa gets to the root cause of your fears—and how to overcome them!"
—Randy Gage, Author of *How to Build a Multi-Level Money Machine*

"There is so much powerful information in this book. It has opened by eyes to a new way of thinking. It has really changed my life and renewed my faith."

—Charles Goubert, Excel Communications

"Finally my search is over! This is a comprehensive and complete plan that provided me bottom line RESULTS for myself and the people on my team I've immediately put in practice the techniques, and have already recruited a True Leader! This book is PURE GOLD, A REAL TREASURE."

—Sherry Cantua, Telewrx Senior Marketing Director

"Fantastic! This book is a jewel! It's drilling down into the pulp where the blood really flows. It hurts like the dickens, but Lisa is telling us the truth in a way that I've never heard before."
—Dr. Beverly Kurtin

"This book really hit me right between the eyes! I've applied it to many areas of my life—not just business—and have seen tremendous results."
—Laura Miller, Creative Memories Senior Unit Leader

"With every read, I gain more insight into myself and am able to fight off the demons of doubt!"
—Johnny, "The Transition Man" Campbell, Professional Speaker

"This book has set me free! I was shocked at how much I saw myself in the chapter on false beliefs. Read this amazing book and finally be free of the limitations that hold you back!"
—Joyce Thomas, The Jade Company

# Dedication

I was standing in the lobby of the San Francisco Marriott, talking with my friend Lee Glickstein, when an adorable two-year-old girl came skipping by, her mother hovering close behind. We could clearly see the excitement and delight in the child's eyes as she ran around the room, giggling happily and savoring every second of this delicious adventure.

Breaking our silent fixation, Lee turned to me and said, "That little girl is you, Lisa, bursting with excitement and finding the sparkle in life!"

Lee was right. That little girl did remind me of myself - with one exception. My mother didn't hover over me when I just had to dig deep into the richness of life. No. She would stand in the middle of my life with a smile of confirmation on her sweet face as she watched me go.

That is why this book is dedicated to my mom, Helen Kelly.

Thank you for always letting me go and grow, for having the confidence and faith that I would be okay.

From the time you and Dad let me go to Central America when I was eleven years old. Those three months in a different culture gave me an invaluably rich experience, one that helped me learn to appreciate the wonderful differences in people and how those differences make life so colorful! Who would have known that I would grow up to speak worldwide on that very topic...

...to the time you supported (with some hesitation) my crazy idea of quitting my first year of college and moving to Hawaii when just eighteen years old. That adventure taught me - with great conviction - that God has a specific plan for me and He will always provide for me.  His timing and provision are all I need. Who would have known that I would grow up to one day graduate with a doctorate degree and help others grow their faith and love God . . .

...to my wedding day where I walked down the isle and then hours later walked on a plane to start my new life with Mark in Florida - 3,000 miles away from you and Dad. Who would have known that we would build a life that we love in Florida and our home would be a place you and Dad come for fun in the Florida sun!

I never knew, until I had three kids of my own, how much you did for me when you gave me the beautiful gift of freedom.

Thank you for letting me grow into the person God intended me to be.  You are my most precious blessing.  I love you.

Your daughter,
Lisa

# Table of Contents

*"To love and be loved is to feel the sun from both sides."*

—David Viscott, M.D.

*"You must do the things you think you cannot do."*

*—Eleanor Roosevelt*

# Acknowledgments

Everything I've ever done in my life that I am truly proud of came about because a lot of wonderful people were there to help. I thank each one of you for your support, belief, and love.

## To my former husband Mark:

Thank you for being such a great dad to our kids. It is because you did so much with the kids that I was able to have the time to write. I was reminded of just how much you did to help me complete this book project every time one of our kids would accidentally call me "Daddy." I'm happy to have been your wife for 15 years.

## To my children:

Auriana, Beau and Connor, you gave me incredible motivation to stay focused and excited about this book project, especially every time we'd walk into the bookstore and you would run to the best-seller list, look through all the titles and shout, "You're not on the list yet, Mom!" I am so happy God chose me to be your mother.

## To the National Speakers Association and Florida Speakers Association:

I love being a member, attending the conventions, and building such great friendships. It is because of you I have found my calling and do what I love to do. Thank you for your example of excellence.

## To Peter Schlosser (The Wild One!):

You are the possibility of Freedom and Fun; my two highest values. Thank you for loving me, taking a stand for me, and holding me to my greatness. You are an amazing man.     Whoooosh!

## To my master-mind group, "The Circle":

Brad Johnson, Steve Siebold, Tom Welch, Randy Gage. Thank you so much for your ingenious ideas and the motivation you gave me for this book project. The accountability aspect of our group has made me a better person. When we are together, there's electricity in the air! You guys are brilliant! Joining this group is the best thing I've done for my career since joining NSA. I'm so glad you're all in my life.

## To my Bible Study Fellowship Group:

Suzanne Comparato, Nancy Doran, Chickie Alexander, Elizabeth Craig, Carla Gates, Nancy Cooke, Laurie Gutches, Gail Howe, Aneria Jackowitz, Kathy Johnsen, Beth O'Donoghue, Andrea Taylor, Margie Vermillion, Sandy Martin, Sandy Sheehy, and our teacher, Linda : Studying God's word with all of you is the single most important thing I do in my life. Thank you for praying for this book project so faithfully. Seeing how God answers the prayers we've placed before Him has built my faith more than I can say. You ladies are what Christians are truly called to be.

## To Donna Sandberg:

Every time I spend time with you, I know my life will be enriched. Your belief in this project is why I was able to stick to it. You and Lauren are my favorite vacation buddies.

## To the wonderful friends and family who kept my focus laser sharp by always asking how the book was going:

Leslie Buterin, Kristin Grassi, Sharon Menzel, Teri Knight, Charlotte Thornton, Cori Crismon, and the "other moms": Gerri Emmets, Gail Howe, Cecilia Peters, Diane Stoller, and Theama Grimm

## To Randy Gage:

You were the person who saw success in me before I could even see it. You were the one who gave me my first big break in speaking. You were the one who designed my book cover, catalog, and marketing materials. You were the one . . . How do you do it?! Your brilliant marketing skill and willingness to share overwhelms me. Above all this, though, it is our precious friendship that I treasure the most. I love that you always seem to bring out the best in me. I'm a better person because I've known you.

## To Dee Robertson:

Your effort with this book project is a gift you gave to each person who reads it.

## To Vicki McCown:

You helped me raise my standards with this project. Your expertise made the difference in creating a high-quality piece.

## To Michael Rosen at Sheridan Books:

You were a big part in turning my manuscript into a published book. Thank you for all you did to make my dream a reality!

## To My Spiritual Leaders

Pastor Mike Potts, The spiritual wisdom I receive from your weekly sermons has helped me become a better person. It is evident that your words are anointed and your life reflects a man who walks closely with Jesus, our Lord. Thank you for your assistance with this book project and your wise council.Dr. Dale Goodman, Thank you for the advice and prayer you gave me on this project. The belief you have in me has lifted me up to heights I didn't know existed! I'm blessed to call you my pastor and friend.

**To my siblings Renee, Chuck, and Scott:**

Growing up with each of you was a privilege. You taught me something valuable that is a part of who I am today. Renee, you taught me to notice detail and the value of organization in life. Chuck, you taught me faith in God and the great sense of humor found in Him. Scott, you taught me to revel in being who you really are and to do what you really love in life. Thank you Scott, for all you do for me! Lisa

*"Life is like riding a bicycle. You don't fall off unless you plan to stop pedaling."*

—Claude Pepper

# *Introduction*

# **Conquer Fear!**

## *Ending Procrastination and Self-Sabotage to Achieve What You Really Want*

Two men enroll in a class on goal-setting. The first man uses what he learns to achieve his goals; the second does not. Instead, he allows fear, lack of focus, lack of time, procrastination, and self-sabotage to destroy his efforts, never accomplishing the very thing he says he wants.

That dilemma—and my experience with it within both my professional and personal life—led me to write this book and program, *Conquer Fear*.

One of the biggest barriers that all salespeople have to overcome is fear. Fear of failure. Fear of rejection. Fear of change. Fear of success. Fear of making decisions. Fear of responsibility. Fear of commitment. It is fear (and all of its cousins, such as worry, anxiety, depression, and self-doubt) that will turn your dream of success into a chilling nightmare that haunts you into paralysis.

But, there is hope! This book is your practical action plan, empowering you to befriend your fear, break through limiting beliefs, and free you to get on with creating success and living the life you love!

In this book, you will learn why positive thinking just isn't enough to instill continuous courage and focus toward your goals. By studying the psychology of success, you will gain great insight in your behavior. You will understand why you do what you do. By practicing visualization techniques you will train your mind to create unstoppable momentum.

There is a missing link... Most books and courses written on this subject address only the psychology factor of fear, neglecting the other important part. The missing link that must be incorporated is the spiritual factor, which is found in faith.

Faith is the opposite of fear. It is faith that fosters courage, boldness, and conviction. Only through faith can we banish fear, anxiety, procrastination, and all the other symptoms that fear creates.

The successful marriage of the dual principles of psychology and spirituality is what makes this book so powerful, what gives you the courage and clarity needed to create lifelong change and significant success.

Yes, you need to know who you are. It is in knowing who you are that you can build on where you want to go. But, you must also know *whose* you are.

This book will guide you in an understanding of whose you are, that God created you to be successful in your purpose. And you already have all you need to make your life work.

The startling truth is: "The only person keeping you from achieving your goals is you." As you move through this book, you will laugh (and be shocked) when you discover the hidden messages your behavior screams out about your belief system, and how your belief system may actually be repelling success.

*Change your beliefs—and you change your behaviors.*

*Change your behaviors—and you change your results.*

*Change your results—and you change your life!*

This is my personal philosophy, one that I bring to every speech, every consultation, and to this book. Through its application, I have seen powerful transformations within people who regain their drive, purpose, childlike courage, commitment, and momentum, who are set on fire as they create career success and a life that they love.

In this book, you will master the steps to change your results and behavior through developing a *powerful belief system*. You will cultivate the kind of faith that can move mountains.

Conquer Fear is your tool for building success. Within its pages you will discover the core truths about goal setting, maintaining focus and motivation, and creating unstoppable momentum.

Learn how to:

- *identify self-limiting beliefs*
- *break through negative programming*
- *conquer procrastination and self-sabotage*
- *raise your self-esteem and confidence level*
- *create more loving relationships*
- *experience more excitement and enjoyment*
- *build momentum to stay motivated and on fire about your goals*
- *raise your success to significance*
- *make your dreams become realities*
- *live a fulfilling life that you love*

By blending the two disciplines of psychology and spirituality—the head and heart aspects of motivation—you will master the strongest method for conquering your fear. You will uncover and understand the reasons behind why you do what you do; you will find your faith and befriend your fear; you will become more courageous and outrageous and finally achieve what you really want.

Whether you are an entrepreneur, a director of a company, a top sales person, a student, a business owner, a parent, a friend—aspire to be one or all of these more effectively—Conquer Fear will show you the way.

*Chapter One*

# What Keeps You From Living Your Dreams?

Newspaper columnist Ann Landers was once asked, "Out of all the thousands of letters you receive each month, what problem is most dominant in people's lives?"

Her answer was shocking! "It's fear!" she replied without hesitation. "The one thing that keeps people from the life they dream of is fear. People live every day in their fear. They're afraid of losing their wealth. They're afraid of losing their loved ones. They're afraid of being themselves. They're afraid of growing up and being responsible. They're afraid of making the wrong decision. They're afraid of making a commitment. They're afraid of life itself!"

Wow! When I pondered that quote I realized that the greatest fear, that keeps my sales force and myself from succeeding, is not fear of failure, but the fear of success. It's the fear of really making it! What people are most fearful of is really living! They fear giving life everything they've got when they don't know the ultimate outcome.

The fear of living to the fullest may have paralyzed you, causing you either to never really try in life or, if you do try, to sabotage your efforts so you never have to face your fear of success! Most people live their life in this fear bondage, and they aren't even aware of its control on them. Fear is the one thing that can turn your dreams of financial freedom, loving relationships, a fulfilling and significant life into a pattern of procrastination, self-sabotage, and other bad habits.

### Truth #1
**Fear is the dominant problem in your life today.**

The two questions I had to answer in order to conquer my fear are the same two questions you will be able to answer after reading this book.

Question one: "Which fear has the most control over me and my behaviors? Is it the fear of failure, fear of rejection, fear of success, or all three?"

Question two: "How do I interrupt the bad habits that I have developed as a means of protection from this fear?"

# The Reality of Fear

Fear is human. It is part of every person's life, exists in every success story, and is part of growing. Fear isn't going away. Some fear is even healthy. In fact, God has a distinct function for fear. It is given to you to keep you safe and to bring you closer to your Creator. Let me explain . . .

All people are born with three inborn fears. These three fears are:

*fear of falling*

*fear of loud noises*

*fear of abandonment*

These inborn fears were given to you to help you monitor what goes on around you. Think about it: It is fear that gives you the powerful adrenaline rush so that you will have the ability to flee from a situation that is truly unsafe or the same adrenaline rush to fight to win! Yes, fear is a gift, instilled in you to keep you safe and lead you to faith. And these three inborn fears were intended as a means of protection, not as a means of destruction.

Fear was intended to bring you to your Creator. Faith is born in fear. God, in His infinite wisdom, knew it would be fear that would propel us back to Him. "The fear of the Lord is the beginning of wisdom," King David wrote.

Take the story of a man named John. A sailor, he served on the high seas since he was eleven years old. His father trained him well for a career as a shipmaster in the Royal Navy. But, even with this great training, he never did make it as an officer. Instead, his bad attitude and his rebellious behavior caused him to be repeatedly demoted and flogged.

In his early twenties, John made his way to Africa, where he got a job on a slave ship, the Greyhound.

As he made the crossings, he would ridicule others—especially the religious. John had no place in his life for God. In fact, he was degrading a book that would eventually help reshape his life, *The Imitation of Christ*, when his ship sailed into an angry storm.

That night the waves pummeled the Greyhound, spinning the ship on the top of a wave and then plunging her deep into the water.

Soon a side of the Greyhound collapsed. John woke to find his cabin filled with water and his ship on the brink of sinking.

For nine hours, he and the other sailors struggled to keep the ship afloat, fearing a losing cause. That night would be their last. This once rebellious man, out of cold fear, finally threw himself on the deck and pleaded with God, "If this will not do, then Lord have mercy on us all."

The legend goes on to tell of the mercy God showed John and his crew even when they didn't deserve mercy. God spared him and the Greyhound.

After surviving the storm, John returned to England where he became a prolific composer. You know his most famous song and probably have sung it countless times:

> *Amazing grace how sweet the sound,*
> *That saved a wretch like me!*
> *I once was lost, but now am found,*
> *Was blind, but now I see.*

This sailor-turned songwriter was John Newton. You would never believe this rebellious man would become one of the greatest hymn writers and preachers of all time. For nearly fifty years, he filled churches with his message of God and his story of grace. What had begun as a prayer of fear resulted in a lifetime of faith.

Sometimes it is only in extreme fear that we will look to God and choose Him. Fear can be a beautiful gift when it brings you to choose God and look to Him for your source of power and peace.

Think of the times in your own life where you turned to God because He was all you had. Those were probably times of extreme fear. Fear gives birth to faith.

### Truth #2
**Fear is a gift that was instilled in you as a means of protection and a way to bring you closer to God.**

## The Distortion of Fear

What happened? What made fear, which was supposed to be a gift, turn into the number one problem in society today? Why do people allow this gift to negatively control their actions, their beliefs, and ultimately their lives? Well, it has a lot to do with making a distinct difference between reacting to fear and acting in fear. It has everything to do with your belief system, what your beliefs are about fear, and what you have been conditioned to believe. Does this sound confusing? It really is quite simple.

First, let's talk about making a distinction between reacting to fear and acting in fear. Typically children react instinctively when confronted by their basic fears. This is appropriate behavior for their age. As adults, however, these same fears that were meant for good cause people to run and even repel success. The problem is, most adults don't make a clear distinction between reacting with instinct and acting with their intellect when dealing with fear. Most people react instinctively to their fear by running from it, ignoring it, sabotaging their efforts, or quitting their pursuit of the very dream they said they wanted so they won't have to face their fear.

Have you run away from a dream? Have you allowed fear to keep you from achieving or even trying what you really want?

## The Common Scenario

In adulthood, the same fear that was intended as a means of protection and to bring you closer to God now causes you to react with excuses, anxiety, sabotage, and self-defeating behaviors because you are not aware of the gift fear can bring you, and you have not been taught how to have power over your fear. As soon as you feel that tightness in your gut, you react instinctively to your fear by either denying it or running from it. You miss the power that comes from acting with your intellect and befriending your fear. You never allow the fear to become the gift it was intended to be.

That's what this book is all about. You will learn to act with your intellect by exposing your true fear (and the self-limiting beliefs they represent) and free yourself, so you can get on with all you are meant to do, have, and be.

### Truth #3
**When you run from or deny your fear, you leave the gift unopened.**

Most people do not receive the gift that comes from facing their fears. They spend all their energy running from, or denying fear. I know because I had been doing this for years... until one amazing day, when I was able to befriend my fear with a simple technique... telling the truth.

## Bermuda Breakthrough

It was nearing the last days of a National Speakers Association conference held on the beautiful island of Bermuda. Like most people at the conference, I was inspired by all the great information and fired up about all the possibilities I was going to act on in my business... or so I thought.

Randy Gage, my friend and business coach, and I were talking together about building my speaking business.

"You could speak to XYZ Company," Randy suggested.

"No," I replied. "I'm better with different types of audiences than that."

"Okay," he said and tried again. "Set your fee at $___ and you could market yourself to the ABC industry."

"No. I need to finish my doctorate before I'm ready for that." I quickly countered.

Again Randy offered another suggestion. "We could market you to the ABC industry and offer consulting as well as keynotes."

That sounded good to me... at first. Then I thought to myself, "I have three children and a husband who isn't too supportive of this career. What would happen if..."

The conversation went on and on like this. I started to sweat, but told myself it was the hot Bermuda sun.

After several of these responses, Randy looked straight in my eyes and said something that sent chills up my spine. "Lisa, you are afraid of success!"

Now, what would your reply be to someone who accused you of being afraid of success? Yep! You guessed it. I argued, "No, I'm not!

What do you know anyway? You don't have the demands of children and you aren't even married!"

Well, Randy is the kind of friend who knows how to read between words and has the courage to say what he sees. So he repeated, "You're afraid of really making it in this business."

After pondering that statement for a long time, I knew he was right. And, boy, can the truth hurt sometimes. Those words struck a painfulcord in me and there's no Band-Aid big enough to cover that kind of wound.

The truth broke me that day and I began to say aloud (to my surprise) all the real reasons I was afraid of making it in my business...

Would I be a good mother with the demands of a successful career? A professional speaker? Ha! Who was I to think I could accomplish great success? After all, I grew up in the era when good girls were seen and not heard. Would I lose my friends? I enjoyed my life and was comfortable. But, was I guilty of being comfortable in my complaining? "I'm too young." "I'm too inexperienced." And, the one insecurity that every successful person encounters from time to time—no matter how irrational—"I'm nothing but a fraud and I'm going to be found out!" I realized I had a tremendous fear of success. The negative beliefs I had attached to my goal were choking my potential and limiting my success.

That day in Bermuda I realized the real problem lay in not exposing the true fear that kept me from success. Sure, I said it was my unsupportive husband, the incredible competition, the lack of investment capital, my children, the economy, the year . . . all these roadblocks were convenient excuses to keep me "safe" from really trying. I could always use these "reasons" and say, "If only it weren't for _____, then I could have made it big!"

But these fears were not the truth. You see, what I was really afraid of was succeeding!

## What Do You Fear?

What about you? Do you fear . . .

| | |
|---|---|
| *commitment?* | *rejection?* |
| *responsibility?* | *not measuring up?* |
| *growing up?* | *loss?* |
| *confrontation?* | *change?* |

I have never met a person who hasn't had to face some degree of fear. In all of the interviews I did for this book, every person had a story about how they, too, had to deal with their fear. What I began to notice is how similar the stories were! The names would change. The circumstances were different. But the fear was the same—and very real.

All of these surface fears keep you from exposing the core fear, the true cause of the anxiety, depression, and destructive behavior that choke your dreams to death. These symptoms of fear can be conquered by exposing the core fear that hides behind them and breaking through the negative beliefs they represent.

# The Two Core Fears

I believe out of all the fears we say we have, we are controlled by only two core fears. It is from these two major fears that all other fears are born: **Fear of success** and/or **Fear of failure**.

The fear of succeeding and then having to maintain that success can be deadly. I believe the fear of success is the most powerful fear over us because it relates directly to the three inborn fears: Fear of falling, fear of loud noises, and fear of abandonment.

The fear of falling is a natural one for successful people. It's easy to believe that once we've achieve success, there's no place to go but down. The fear of loud noises correlates to sudden change. Perhaps we've been working toward something for months, and then, overnight it seems, something comes through and suddenly we are successful. The fear of abandonment is very real. We might lose some friends after we become successful. They might be jealous of our success, view us as arrogant, or feel that we just don't fit in to the "old group" anymore. We've all heard "It's lonely at the top," and our inborn fear of abandonment is challenged.

When we confront our true fears, we are on our way to freedom.

### Truth #4
**When your fear of success or fear of failure is exposed, you break through their control over you.**

Read the fears on the next page. Circle the fears that you can identify with the most. Then number the fears you've circled in order of their power over you, with the number one being the most powerful.

| | |
|---|---|
| commitment | rejection |
| responsibility | not measuring up |
| growing up | loss |
| confrontation | change |
| 1. | 5. |
| 2. | 6. |
| 3. | 7. |
| 4. | 8. |

If you experience fear of commitment, responsibility, growing up, or change, your core fear is the **fear of success**. If most of your anxiety comes from the fear of rejection, confrontation, or not measuring up, your core fear is the **fear of failure**. Now look at the order of your fears and evaluate which one controls you and holds you back the most. Is it fear of failure or fear of success, or both? Think about what you say out loud or to yourself most often. What you say and think represents your beliefs about success or failure.

The following are the most common negative beliefs for the person who fears failure:

**fear of rejection, fear of confrontation, or fear of not measuring up**
*This has got to be right.*
*I could really make it if I had _____.*
*If I say no, people won't like me.*
*I just can't say no.*
*My life is a soap opera and I'm the star!*
*"They" are out to get me.*
*You can't make me.*
*If I don't finish, then I won't fail.*
*I work better under pressure.*
*All great ideas are already invented.*
*I have nothing valuable to offer.*
*Anything worth doing is worth doing perfectly.*

The following are the most common negative beliefs for the person who fears success:

**fear of commitment, fear of responsibility or fear of growing up**

*If you can't say anything nice, don't say anything at all.*

*If I succeed at this, they'll expect everything I do to be a success.*

*People expect a lot from me.*

*Success has to be hard.*

*To be seen as important, you must have problems.*

*I don't even want to know, then I won't have to commit.*

*I don't want to look too successful; people might call me egotistical.*

*To be focused means you have to commit.*

*It's lonely at the top.*

*This is too hard.*

*This will take too long.*

*I don't want to do what I don't like to do.*

*Successful people don't have to do "this."*

When you can identify your core fear, it is the beginning of your breakthrough. But...there's more!

## Exposing The Beliefs Behind Failure And Success

If you're like most people, you find success terrifying. Yes, success! You may fear writing that best seller, becoming the top salesperson, committing to marriage (and staying married), or succeeding in your business.

When you do make it, when you succeed in accomplishing your goal, you are at the top. When you are at the top, there is nowhere to go but down—or so you believe. The thought of going beyond your first success, or just maintaining that success, can be crippling.

It's not the fear of failure that keeps us from our full potential. No, I believe the fear of really making it is much more frightening. Think

15

of the high school boy who is scared to ask a girl out on a date. Is his fear that she might say no and turn him down? No! What he's really afraid of is: What if she says YES? Or the woman who wants to lose twenty pounds but never makes the commitment to begin and stick with it—not because she might fail, but because she might succeed! Then what? She'd have the pressure of maintaining the weight loss! Yikes! It's easier to just never make the commitment. Or the sales associate who achieves high sales in his unit and now is faced with upholding that achievement, or worse yet, beating it!

If you're like me, you are probably asking yourself, "Where did these fears of success and failure come from?" These two core fears are learned fears that have come about by negative, self-limiting beliefs.

### Truth #5
**Your belief system is the driving force behind your behaviors and your results.**

I knew there had to be something else behind my fear that was the cause of such great anxiety, frustration, procrastination, and low self-confidence. I realized that it isn't just the fear itself that was choking my success. Something bigger was triggering that fear.

As I put my energy into understanding the basis for my fear, I discovered two important clues. First, I realized that fear is relative. What may be fearful to me is not in the least bit fearful to you. From that knowledge I deduced that our fears are a direct reflection of our beliefs, or lack of beliefs. What was triggering my fear was a self-limiting, negative belief system. The great "ah-ha" came when I realized that fear is a by-product of a negative belief.

Read on to discover how the beliefs you hold right now are the very cause of your lack of success...

*"You know what a person thinks not when he tells you what he thinks, but by his actions."*

—Isaac Bashevis Singer

*"All the significant battles are waged within the self."*

—*Sheldon Kopp*

*Chapter 2*
# The Power of Your Belief System

You may be asking, "Come on, Lisa, do my beliefs really have that much power over my behaviors?" I would respond emphatically, "Yes!"

Your beliefs are the driving force behind your behaviors. Beliefs send powerful messages to your brain that affect your actions (and their outcome) in either a positive or negative way. Your beliefs will cause you to do one of two things:

*be fearful and RETREAT, or*

*be empowered and ACT*

Think of the immigrant who has been raised with the belief that America is the land of opportunity. Even before coming to this country, he has the advantage. Once he arrives in America, he begins a business with the conviction that in America he will be successful because that's what he has heard and believes. His beliefs are his reality. With time, he manifests that conviction and becomes successful in his business.

That's how powerful your beliefs are. Success takes two ingredients: belief and time. The more belief you have, the less time it takes. Your belief system causes you to either retreat and repel success, or to act and attract opportunity and success.

Your belief system was "taught" to you by society, peers, family, life experiences, environment, and many other smaller influences. Just think back to what your family said repeatedly concerning your circumstances or your life, and you will find the beginning of many of your beliefs.

# The Making Of A Belief System

## 1. Parents and Family

Remember the countless times as a child you heard: "You're gonna fall!" "You'll put your eye out!" "Slow down!" "I told you you'd get hurt!" I know parents need to guide their children away from danger. But, most parents overemphasize safety and demonize risk-taking by too often inflicting the message of their own fears.

Wouldn't it be great if we parents warned our kids of the danger by saying: "Be safe." "You're safe." "You'll be fine." "Be alert!" "Notice things." These statements help build a positive, empowering belief system about life and our children's capability to handle whatever comes their way.

## 2. Society's Influence

Society has a huge impact on our belief system. Look at Titanic, a movie watched by more people than any other film ever made. Its depiction of wealthy and poor people helped create dangerous, negative belief systems. Wealthy people were portrayed as rude, boring, wicked people who would shoot each other to save their own lives. The picture also reinforced a huge negative belief about love and commitment, as the main character, Kate, planned to marry for money, not for love. We witness her mother telling her to toughen up, because that was what their situation required her to do. Another strong negative belief the movie put forth was that poor people knew how to have a good time and poverty was the answer to Kate's problems.

*Negative belief:*

> *People of wealth are evil, rude, and obnoxious.*
>
> *Money is evil.*
>
> *Poor people are more loving than rich people.*
>
> *It's "spiritual" to be poor.*

## 3. Life Circumstances

*Marilyn's Story:*

I don't want to be successful again because it hurt so badly the first time.

I participated in the triathlon at the 1976 Olympic games and won a medal. "Wow!" I thought to myself as I boarded the plane to come home from the Olympics. "I'm the first woman triathlon champion of the United States of America." I guess I thought my friends, family, and colleagues would react the same way. But, much to my chagrin, I was hit with something quite different.

"Did you get to meet Mark Spitz?" was the repeated question I heard over and over. That hurt so much. It hurt enough for me to know that success isn't for me.

> *Negative belief:*
>
> *Success hurts.*
>
> *It's lonely at the top.*
>
> *Women should not be successful (athletes/business people).*
>
> *Girls should be seen and not heard.*

What about you? What family saying, life circumstance, or society influence has shaped and molded your belief system? We've all had a lot of negative programming, whether we're conscious of it or not. But, it matters less where these negative beliefs were taught and more that *you are aware of them and learn how to break through them.*

23

It is the beliefs you have about success that creates an incredible—very real, very evident—fear of success. This kind of fear is the most powerful form of bondage. This fear-bondage—rooted by negative beliefs about success and failure—is the one thing that will cause you to sabotage your success and never achieve what you really want. No amount of money or time spent on goal-setting classes or positive-thinking techniques will help you create success until you break through the negative beliefs that your fear represents.

The good news is that you have control over your beliefs. You can change your belief system, which will help you conquer your fear forever! Read on to find out how.

## Identify Negative Belief Barriers

Do you ever make any of the following statements?

*"I'm too old."*

*"I'm too young."*

*"There's never enough time."*

*"Love hurts."*

*"There are no good men left."*

*"I don't deserve that."*

*"I work better under pressure."*

*"Successful people are always busy."*

*"Selling is hard."*

*"I can't lose weight."*

*"Millionaires are selfish."*

*"Successful people are bad parents."*

*"My relationships never work."*

*"I can't save."*

*"All great ideas have been shared."*

*"Sales people are pushy."*

*"Everyone will laugh."*

*"I'm not good enough."*

*"We can't do it this way."*

*"Women don't hold those titles."*

*"Chocolate is bad."*

*"If it's not one thing, it's another."*

*"If you can't say anything nice, don't say anything at all."*

*"Children (girls) should be seen and not heard."*

*"Woman should be modest and humble."*

*"You're so smart. If only you'd apply yourself."*

*"Anything worth doing is worth doing perfectly."*

*"Money doesn't grow on trees."*

These negative belief barriers are powerful motivators that will actually cause you to repel success. You will just push it away like a child refuses spinach. The problem isn't just your fear. No, your fear represents a powerful, self-limiting belief! Until your beliefs are identified and replaced with empowering beliefs, no amount of positive thinking will help you create and attain success.

What makes negative beliefs so powerful and so insidious is that most of the time you don't even realize you have them. You will say you want something, you'll write it down, you'll back it up with positive thinking, but then *something happens to keep you from the very thing you say you want*. You'll start misplacing important items. You'll procrastinate on deadlines. You'll forget names. You'll miss an opportunity... the list goes on and on.

*Linda's story:*

Growing up I always heard my parents say, "If it's not one thing, it's another." This seemingly harmless phrase was so imbedded in thought processes that it was affecting my ability to accomplish tasks—not to mention enjoy life. I always felt overburdened. Every little thing seemed to overwhelm me. I always said, "There's not enough time in the day." I knew I had to break through this negative behavior and stop this insanity of constantly feeling defeated and incapable.

*The negative belief:*

*There's never enough time.*

*If it's not one thing, it's another.*

*I don't have what it takes.*

*Life is hard.*

# Expose Self-sabotaging Behavior

The first step to your breakthrough is to listen to what you say and watch what you do. What comes out of your mouth is very reflective of what you believe.

*Truth #6*

**Your everyday habits are broadcasting your belief system, your fear, and your unmet needs loud and clear.**

Your behaviors are broadcasting hidden messages of negative beliefs, fear, and unmet needs.

First, I'll address unmet needs. Psychology explains that behind every behavior lies a reason. Freud said, "We are insatiable beings and we always get our needs met." We will get these needs met in a healthy, conscious way, or we will get them met in an unhealthy, subconscious way.

So, what does all this mean? Human beings have four innate needs. The degrees to which you need these vary with your personality and who you are.

Our four innate needs are:

*attention (love)*      *control*

*excitement*      *solitude*

As you read through the following stories, identify which one are most important to you. Think about how you have been getting each of the following needs met—whether in a healthy or unhealthy way.

## You need more attention (love)

When you need more attention and you're not getting it on a healthy level, you will subconsciously behave in a way that will get that need met. You may start losing your keys or important papers. You may get hurt or fall ill often. When you suffer these setbacks, what happens to you and the people around you? You guessed it! Other people come to your aid, helping you find your missing keys, comforting you in your pain, or taking care of you while you're ill. You receive the attention you need.

One day, after my husband, Mark, misplaced his keys for the third time that week, I began to make more time for him. I made eye contact with him for longer lengths of time. I asked him more questions and listened more. The outcome was amazing! He acted differently. He was more relaxed and seemed to focus on tasks more carefully. He remembered where he placed items and things were back to normal in our home.

If you enjoy being in the spotlight and the center of attention, and you are not receiving this recognition, other behaviors could surface. Some people continuously get hurt—either physically or emotionally. I had a client named Sally with whom I was conducting family consultation. She would come every week, recalling incredibly sad stories of her family, her job, and her health. It seemed nothing ever went right for Sally. My heart broke for her.

One day after sharing one of her heartbreaking stories, Sally said, "My life is a soap opera, and I am the STAR!" Without realizing it, Sally had made a profound discovery. She was getting a huge need met through her negative situations. Since life did not give her the attention she so desperately wanted—and needed—she became her own "star" in her life dramas. Yes, bad things happen to all people, but when they become a way of life, the question must be asked whether the person is creating that negative drama.

There's a great end to that story. When I suggested she work on her own personal development and life interests, she finally found a way to receive the attention and the confidence she needed, without creating traumatic events in her life.

## You need more excitement

If you are a person who values adventure and loves excitement—and are not getting it—you may be meeting this need through the adrenaline rush that comes from being late or overextending yourself. I'm proud to say I am a person who loves excitement and adventure. I am not proud to say I fall into the trap of the unhealthy ways of feeding that need.

Picture this: I'm getting ready for work. I'm on time today. In fact, I'm ten minutes early. So, what do I do? Do I sit down and relax, pray, or maybe read a little? No! I start a new project that gets me so involved, I lose track of time and cause myself to be (you guessed it) late! Why do I do that?

I do it because I love the adrenaline rush that being late gives me. I'm addicted to the charge that I get from dashing around doing the last-minute things that get my blood pumping, puts a jump in my step, but also makes me crazy, unproductive, and irritable!

What about you? Do you wait for the last possible day to work on a project that should have taken you three days? Do you wait until April 14th to begin collecting your tax information? It could be because you love the adrenaline rush that you get from last-minute pressures.

While studying for my doctorate, I read a case about a chronic procrastinator. Although this man had an incredible need for adventure and excitement, his life was filled with deadlines and structure. So, he got his need met in an unhealthy way—by running his business and personal life on a last-minute basis. He was a chronic procrastinator! To fulfill the man's need for excitement, his doctor prescribed that he take up skydiving!

I'm not suggesting you pick up skydiving, but I am suggesting you fill your weeks with activities that excite you in order to get this need met on a healthy basis.

## You need more control

When you need more control over your life, you will behave in ways to gain more control. Often, these ways can be unhealthy and not beneficial.

Another woman I counseled used to wait until the last minute to pay her bills. She had the money in her checking account, but would not write the check until the very last minute, which caused her to often be late on her bills. She couldn't figure out why she wouldn't write out the checks earlier until she faced this control issue. "I feel like I'm getting ripped off." she admitted "I don't want to give them the money until I'm ready to."

When she changed her belief about paying her bills, she realized she was grateful for the service. She also began to see that she had the ultimate control of credit cards. She didn't have to use them. But if she did, she would pay the monthly bill without resentment knowing it was a privilege and her choice to use the convenience of credit.

If you are a person who needs more control, try reevaluating your beliefs about what control you do have. Afterwards, begin exercising that control. Say no to tasks when you have too much on your plate, so you can say yes to those things you really want to (and should) be doing.

Reevaluate your beliefs about control. Come to grips with what you do have control over—and choose to release everything else.

## You need more solitude

Beth got home before her husband that evening. She was tired from all the demands at work and looking forward to some time alone. When Tim came home, Beth immediately instigated an argument. The next thing she knew, the argument had escalated and she found herself saying "I'm going for a walk" as she slammed the door behind her.

"What just happened?" she wondered to herself. She couldn't even remember what she was angry about.

Look back at Beth's behavior. She got exactly what she wanted. She was alone. When you need more alone time, you will behave in ways to get it. Usually, these ways are unhealthy and not beneficial. What Beth should have done is told the truth (without guilt) by saying, "I need a half hour to myself, Tim. I'll be in the bedroom (or outside or in the bath) to unwind and regroup."

The magical key here is to get your needs met on a healthy, conscious basis. Start telling the truth to your spouse, your colleagues, and yourself! Being chronically late, overextending yourself, and even instigating an argument could be your red flag of warning. When you tell the truth about what your innate needs are, and find healthy ways to get those needs met, you will be freed to live more congruently with who God made you to be. When you have the courage to ask for what you need—from your friends, your family, your boss, yourself—you give others the permission to meet their innate needs as well.

Look at your behaviors. They are shouting out messages of unmet needs and hidden fears.

When you find yourself procrastinating, forgetting appointments, not taking advantage of opportunities, or any other sabotage behavior, know that these actions are revealing your fear. Fear is directly related to negative beliefs. These beliefs cause you to react to a problem instead of respond to it. Negative belief systems are powerful motivators that control your behaviors. These signs of self-sabotage occur every day in the life of a person who is controlled by their fears and the negative beliefs they represent.

If you are saying one thing . . .

*"I want to have an intimate relationship."*

*"I want to become double diamond."*

*"I want to get a doctorate degree."*

*"I want to take this promotion in my company."*

*"I want to become financially secure."*

*"I want less stress in my life."*

*"I want more fun in my family life."*

...but your actions (what you do daily) reveal a different message ...

*You get sick the day before your big date.*

*You choose people who are unable to make commitments.*

*You misplace an important file.*

*You aren't making the number of sales calls you know you need to in order to succeed.*

*You procrastinate often and miss deadlines or have to rush and submit poor quality work.*

*You don't respond to opportunity around you or you aren't even aware of it.*

*You show up late for work or important meetings.*

. . . then you are a victim of self-sabotage.

Self-sabotage is a reflection of your fears caused by negative beliefs. It occurs when you link fear (fueled by negative beliefs) to your goals.

Learn to look at your behaviors. Start by reviewing the following most common forms of self-sabotage. These behaviors are all red flags announcing your hidden fears and negative beliefs. In what ways are you sabotaging your success?

# Examples Of Five Self-sabotaging Behaviors

*Behavior # 1: Procrastination*

*Behavior # 2: Disorganization*

*Behavior # 3: Rebelliousness / Anger*

*Behavior # 4: Busyness / Lack of Productivity & Focus*

*Behavior # 5: Perfectionism / Overpleaser*

## 1. Behavior # 1: Procrastination

*James's story:*

James had a meeting set on Friday with an important prospective client. He wanted to put together a killer proposal that would ensure a signed contract.

On Tuesday, he wrote on his to-do list "Do research for proposal." When he looked at those words that night, he was shocked that he had totally forgotten about it.

On Wednesday morning he sat at his desk writing out that day's to-do list. He had over twenty-three items on the list, so he knew he couldn't write the proposal today at work. No, he needed a relaxed, calm setting to write this perfect, dynamic proposal. He would find time to write it tonight when he had no interruptions.

On Friday morning around 2 a.m., after working on the proposal for over three hours, he printed the finished product, turned off the computer, and dragged himself to bed, hoping that his verbal skills would overcome the poorly written proposal.

### Examples of Behavior:

You put off taking initiative on a task you must perform to accomplish your goal. You wait until the last minute to do an important task.

### Self-Limiting Belief:

I work better under pressure.

I don't want to do what I don't like to do.

I should do this because _____ thinks I should.

### Hidden Fear:

Afraid of Success.

You are addicted to the adrenaline rush that comes from waiting until the last minute and then forging full speed ahead to complete the task.

You link too much pain to accomplishing the goal and becoming successful. You're afraid of the changes you will have to make because of the success.

What you're working toward is not really your dream. It's someone else's. But you're so deep into it now you don't know how to stop, tell the truth, and get out of what you're doing and on to something you really love.

## 2. Behavior # 2: Disorganization—Lack of Focus

*Karen's story:*

Karen couldn't find a thing in that mess. She spent so much of her time and energy looking for important files and phone numbers that she was exhausted by 10 a.m. She decided to take drastic measures. She hired a professional organizer. Karen learned a lot about organization, and she got a lot out of the system that the professional organizer taught her. There was a still a problem, however.

Karen would not discipline herself to follow the new system, and in several days things were just as disorganized as times before. Even after the time and money spent on a professional organizer, Karen still lacked focus.

### Example of Behavior:

You misplace important papers, files, numbers, and belongings. You spend a lot of your time looking for these lost items. You have not created a system; or, if you have, you don't follow it. You don't keep a good accounting system. You are not focused.

### Self-limiting belief:

Success has to be hard.

To be seen as important I must have problems.

I can always find things in this mess. Besides, I work better with chaos.

If I don't finish, then I won't fail.

I don't even want to know, then I won't have to commit.

I don't want to look too successful, people might call me egotistical.

To be focused means I have to commit.

It's lonely at the top.

### Hidden Fear:

Afraid of Success

You believe success has to be really hard, so you attract more problems than you really have. You think to have problems means you look successful.

You are scared to death to get committed to a project, a relationship, or a responsibility of any kind. You are afraid of what would happen if you got really serious toward something and succeeded.

"Don't do it too good or people will be jealous and not like you" is one of your beliefs. You don't want people to think you're pretentious. So, you once in a while make sure you look a mess and not too successful.

You are afraid to be responsible to anyone because you don't want to let them down. If you don't make any commitments, then you won't ever have to grow up.

You are living someone else's dream for your life. You're so used to doing what others tell you, you don't even realize you don't know what you want.

## 3. Behavior # 3: Rebelliousness—Anger

*Rick's Story:*

Rick hired me to help him with his presentation skills. He wanted to grow his financial business through offering public seminars. He had already held a few seminars with disastrous results. After I reviewed his material and spent some time with him, I knew that his presentation skills were not the cause of his failed seminars. Rather, Rick was plagued by negative beliefs about public speakers. These negative beliefs were controlling his ability to succeed in these seminars!

I asked him to write down all the connotations he had of the concept "financial planner." I saw there were only positive connotations to that word. Great! But, when I asked him to list all the words he could relate to the concept "public speaker", amazingly he wrote phrases like, "speakers are arrogant," "speakers are untruthful," "speakers are untrustworthy and sly." There it was! His subconscious could not allow him to succeed at these seminars because of his negative beliefs about public speakers. Rick needed to replace the negative beliefs he had about speaking with empowering ones before he could attract and create success.

When you have negative beliefs about your role, you will inevitably attach fear to your goal. And no amount of money or time spent on goal-setting workshops will ever cure you until you identify the negative beliefs behind the fear.

## Examples of Behavior:

You connect pain, loss of control, or loss of self to your goal. Even though you say you want to achieve this goal, you actually repel opportunity so you won't have to experience this pain and negative connotation.

You see deadlines, bills and taxes as signs of authority. You hold off paying bills to control your money. You rebel against a deadline because it is a symbol of control over you.

## Self-Limiting Belief:

I don't want to do what I don't like to do.

"They" are out to get me.

You can't make me.

Successful people don't have to do "this."

People expect too much from me.

## Hidden Fear:

Afraid of Failure

You are afraid of being out of control. You put something off that you say you really want because then you feel that you have control over "them." Your goal is not congruent with your beliefs.

## 4. Behavior # 4: Busy But Unproductive

*Tim's Story:*

Tim is excited. He just began a new business with a direct marketing company. He read the literature on the company and the product and says he's ready to go. But, he doesn't begin calling on his prospect list.

"I really should learn a little bit more about the company before I begin," he says to his sponsor. "I need to try all the products before I start selling them."

"Okay," replies his sponsor, "let's say you've read up on the company and you tried all the products. Now what?"

Tim began to feel uncomfortable as he pictured himself "selling" the products. Soon he sensed what his sponsor was getting at. He was allowing his "perfection" to get in the way of his success. Together, they got to the core of Tim's beliefs about selling and the fear those beliefs were causing.

"I just don't want people to think I'm being pushy," Tim finally admitted. "Sales people push their product on others without knowing if the product would really help them."

Some people make themselves very busy so they won't have to focus on completing the one thing that they are called to do—the one thing that would ensure their success. If they don't ever have to make the time to do the project, then they always have the excuse that they were just too busy.

Examples of Behavior:

Your schedule is overloaded. You are into everything. You love to try different things, to experience a lot of diversity. You get bored easily, so you often don't finish projects before moving on to the next new, exciting one. You say yes to everyone who asks for your help. You sometimes cause arguments (pick fights) and you don't know what you're angry about.

Self-Limiting Belief:

There's never enough time.

Successful people look busy

If I say no, people won't like me.

I just can't say no.

My life is a soap opera, and I'm the star!

If it's not one thing, it's another.

Hidden Fear:
  Afraid of Success / Afraid of Failure

If you commit to one thing, you are terrified of getting bored with it. If you complete tasks within ample time, you would miss the adrenaline rush you receive from procrastinating.

You believe you need to look busy to be successful, so you occupy yourself with little tasks, but never get to the one thing you really need to complete. You lack direction and focus because you have negative beliefs and negative connotations attached to your goal.

You say yes to everyone who asks things of you. You just can't say no because you don't want to let anybody down or make it seem as though you can't handle things. But, in reality, when you say yes to everyone who asks something of you, you actually take away from your success. When you say yes to a job that someone else is supposed to perform you actually take away the blessing that they would have (and should have) received.

## 5. Behavior # 5: Perfectionism—Overpleaser

Examples of Behavior:
  You read and reread training manuals and don't begin the process until you master the training. You avoid confrontation. You would do almost anything to appease an angry client, friend, or spouse.

Self-limiting Belief:
  This has got to be right.
  I'm good at this. This should be easy.
  If you can't say anything nice, don't say anything at all.
  Anything worth doing is worth doing perfectly.
  If I succeed at this, they'll expect everything I do to be a success.
  I could really make it if I only had _____.

Hidden Fear:
  Afraid of Failure

You fear making a mistake and being "found out" that you make mistakes and aren't perfect. You fear being out of control of a situation and losing face or being rejected by others. You fear getting "dirty" and not looking like you have it together.

You hate conflict. You don't take a leadership position because you want people to like you so much. You won't break through this until you stop fearing people and what they think of you. I once heard a pastor say that until we lose our fear of people and attain a fear of God, we will never live life to the fullest.

What is the hidden message of fear your behavior is broadcasting? When you identify the self-limiting beliefs that cause these negative behaviors (self-sabotage), you break the bondage that they have over you. Tell the truth. Tell it to a stranger. Tell it to a loved one. Tell it to yourself, but identify the self-limiting beliefs relentlessly, and, in doing so, you will be set free from their bondage.

## Self-limiting Belief:

I don't deserve that.

Selling is hard.

If something is worth doing, it's worth doing perfectly.

You don't consciously realize you are sabotaging your success—but your actions and behaviors reveal the truth. The one major symptom of fear and negative beliefs is self-sabotage.

Self-sabotage is a disparity between what you say you want and what your actions show. Your subconscious mind is powerful. Its job is to keep you safe. So, when it detects fear caused by a negative belief, it will do anything to keep you from achieving your goals. When you attach fear to your goal, your subconscious will do its job, keeping you safe and repelling anyone and anything that would cause you to succeed. It is when your fear (and the negative beliefs it represents) overcomes your desire that you will sabotage your success.

Do you ever procrastinate on the very things that will ensure your success? Have you ever lost a client's contact information or misplaced an important file? Have you ever picked a fight with someone and you can't even really remember why you were so angered? Have you ever gained a lot of weight? Have you ever waited till the last minute to accomplish an important task?

Why do we do these kinds of things? Why do we intentionally cause ourselves stress and grief, especially when we say we don't want to behave that way? When our goals (pictures of success) are not congruent with our beliefs, fear and all its relatives (anxiety, procrastination, sabotage and worry) begin to set in and choke our success.

You can stop your saboteur behavior by identifying and breaking through the negative belief that is causing your fear. It's not really procrastination, or lack of organization, or rebelliousness, or busyness, or perfection that is stifling your success. It is fear and your negative beliefs that are motivating and fueling your sabotage behavior. These behaviors are not the problem. They are the symptoms of the problem. When you face your fear and change the negative beliefs they represent, you will put an end to sabotaging behavior forever!

Read on to find out how to stop the insanity of self-sabotage and all the other behaviors that are keeping you from achieving your goals.

*"If you think you can, you can. And, if you think you can't, you're right."*

*—Mary Kay Ash*

## *Chapter 3*
# Break Through Self-Limiting Beliefs That Prevent Your Success

You do have control over what you believe. Beliefs are like jackets. If one doesn't fit you, you can take it off and put one on that suits you better. But first you must identify and admit your negative beliefs and the fear they represent.

I know this can be hard to take. I certainly found it difficult that day in Bermuda and the months following when I had to face my fear and identify the negative beliefs my fear represented. You may be thinking, "How could this happen to me? I'm using all the techniques I learned in my goal-setting class. I'm thinking positively and visualizing my success." While all those things are important—and we will be covering those very things later in the book—you first need to know that your belief system is more powerful than your positive thinking and visualization techniques. You see, as important as those strategies are, they deal with the head. The way to create lifelong change is to deal with the heart. Fear, and the beliefs they represent, need both a head and heart transformation.

You are not alone in facing this challenge. All people on the road to success have to face their negative belief system. The successful person has just simply learned that the only thing keeping them from achieving their goals is what they choose to believe and what they choose to think. The core message of this book is: Only you have control over your thoughts and your beliefs. When you choose to adopt an empowering belief system and transform your way of thinking, you have mastered the combination for lifelong success.

*Truth # 7:*
**Change your beliefs and you change your behaviors.**
**Change your behaviors and you change your results.**
**Change your results and you change your life.**

# Bermuda Breakthrough Continues

Later that day in Bermuda I tried an exercise that changed my career. I took out a sheet of paper and wrote the word "Millionaire" across the top of the page. Then I listed all the connotations I had in my belief system to that word.

What came out shocked me! I wrote, "Millionaires are selfish." "Millionaires are so busy they aren't good parents." "Millionaires are not faithful." Where did this come from? The reason I was having difficulty became obvious. My subconscious was actually repelling success in order to protect me. Why? Because of all those negative beliefs and pain I had connected to achieving that goal. This wasn't just a light bulb going off in my head; it was an entire Fourth of July fireworks display. The "oohs" and "ahhs" became a glorious "Aha!" Breaking through, I realized the need to take steps to change those negative beliefs.

I began by calling my husband from Bermuda and sharing all my fears and reasons I had not allowed myself to move forward. I went as far to say that I was using his "lack of support" as my way of not having to really try. His response was, "Thank God you finally see it!"

When I returned home, I stepped off the plane to Mark holding a bouquet of flowers and a card that read, "I love you. Now, let's get to work!" It was one of those teary airport scenes we've all seen a million times. I happily realized he wasn't the uncaring tyrant I had accused him of being (or wanted him to be.)

## Adopting Empowering Beliefs

When I returned to work, I knew it was imperative for me to begin changing my beliefs about success. I had to attach positive connotations to being successful. I posted the quote "Money gives you choices." I thought of every example I knew of successful people helping others and using their success for the power of good. I posted a personal quote that I began living my life by this simple principle:

*Change your beliefs and you change your behaviors.*

*Change your behaviors and you change your results.*

*Change your results and you change your life.*

I completed the breakthrough I began in Bermuda with the following exercise. I made a poster showing pictures of all the positive connotations I could think of for the concept of "success." I could help my church spread the Gospel. I could help an aspiring speaker. I could travel with my family and teach my children about different cultures. The one possibility that stirred me the most was, I could treat my mom to a vacation in Hawaii. Just the two of us!

When I began to change the beliefs and attach positive connotations to my goal of being a successful speaker, my career soared. I used the power of vision to keep me motivated on a daily basis. I pasted inspiring pictures of the places we wanted to visit, I wrote down the names of the foundations I could help support, and I hung the outfit (outside my closet) I would wear on the plane to Hawaii!

Just nine months after that life-changing breakthrough, I had more dates on my calendar than I have ever had in my career. I felt great when I gave my church enough money to help them buy cappuccino machines for their college ministry. It enjoyed sending money to people (sometimes anonymously) at a time when I knew they could really use it. But, the best feeling of all was wearing the outfit that hung outside my closet for so long and spending five incredible days with my mom in Hawaii!

What made the difference? How did I change my life so soon? Quite simply, I changed my beliefs, which transformed my way of thinking. My procrastination, sabotage, worry, and other behaviors were signs of my negative beliefs. I knew I couldn't stop these habits until I changed the belief behind them. Saying things like "just stop procrastinating," and "think positively" were not enough.

Sometimes I would stop procrastinating for a while. But, because I didn't deal with my fear by changing the negative belief it represented, I would find another form of sabotage to hinder my success. It was a vicious, exhausting circle. When I began to change my beliefs about success, myself, my life, and God, then my behaviors began to change automatically. Self-limiting beliefs are learned behaviors. And anything learned can be unlearned. Behaviors can only be changed when you change the beliefs that cause them and transform your way of thinking.

Your entry into this life-changing journey begins with listing all your negative beliefs and replacing each one with empowering truth.

## 1. Old Belief: There's never enough time.

### New Belief: God in His infinite wisdom made twenty-four hours enough time.

There is always enough time to do what you really want to do. People who prioritize learn to say no, have clear goals, and find enough time to get the most important things accomplished. There is no such thing as time in eternity. Start to think "abundance" and you will retrain your mind to believe that there is always enough time.

## 2. Old Belief: I work better under pressure.

### New Belief: I work best when I allow suitable time to complete tasks.

You may believe your work quality is enhanced when you are motivated by pressure. However, it could be you are addicted to the rush that comes from working and living like this. If you had ample time to complete a project, you would be overwhelmed at the improvement and heightened creativity.

## 3. Old Belief: There's always something.

### New Belief: There's a solution to every problem.

Most people would rather live in a whirlwind of turmoil than in a boring life. If you are like most, you may be attracting problems because it makes you feel that your life is important. While problems do exist on your road to success, they are not a curse put on you. Everyone has problems. You need to view your problems in a different way. They are just a part of life. Don't exaggerate their power or allow them to be your excitement in life.

## 4. Old Belief: Anything worth doing is worth doing perfectly.

### New Belief: Anything worth doing is worth failing-forward at, until I get it right.

Microsoft giant, Bill Gates, has a curious rule in his company. He tells his people that unless their idea has been laughed at three times, it is not creative enough.

Tom Watson of IBM once hired a man to take care of the company's investment portfolio. On one occasion, this man lost the company millions of dollars. When the unlucky employee approached the CEO to give his resignation, Mr. Watson looked at him and said, "You just cost this company millions of dollars educating you. You are the last person leaving this company!"

These corporate giants have different views of failure. Like them, you need to rethink your definition of failure and view it as priceless education.

## 5. Old Belief: If I say no, people won't like me.

### New Belief: When I say no to some opportunities, I can say yes to better ones.

What was one of the first words you ever learned? Probably the word no. You used that word often in childhood because it gave you power. The word still holds power for you in adulthood. It can keep you safe, by allowing you to decline a proposition that you know is not in your best interest. It can ensure balance in your life, by helping you not to overextend yourself. Using the word no keeps you dedicated to your commitments when, tempted by the lure of getting off course, you say no to the temptation and stay on track. When you respect the word no, allow yourself and others to use it, you discover freedom.

## 6. Old Belief: Successful people are always busy.

### New Belief: Successful people live a life they love and are at peace with.

Every morning you watch this woman in a business suit dash in your local Starbucks for her morning double-espresso-cappuccino. Her cell phone rings continuously as she waits impatiently for her legal stimulant. After tossing in several sugar packets and stirring ferociously, she frantically runs to her car to attend to her busy life.

You think to yourself, "She must be successful."

Too often, society equates success with being busy. In reality, the successful person is the one who lives a balanced life.

## 7. Old Belief: If you want something done right, you've got to do it yourself.

### New Belief: If you want something done right, give it to the one who can best do it.

It may be difficult for you to delegate because you think you'll lose control. You would rather overwork yourself then relinquish power. However, when you surround yourself with competent people and allow them to do their job, you not only grant yourself the freedom to complete your task with single-minded focus, you also give yourself the privilege of watching others shine in their talents.

Adopt these new beliefs and make them your own. Copy them on index cards, or rewrite them in your own words and your own truth and post them in your office, car, and home. Meditate on them throughout the day and plant them in your heart. Surround yourself with truth, and you will shatter your self-limiting beliefs and be free to live each day to your fullest potential.

*"The truth of the matter is that you always know the right thing to do. The hard part is doing it."*
—*General H. Norman Schwarzkopf*

# Chapter 4

# Creating Your Powerful Belief System

Your belief system can be compared to legs holding up a table. The more belief you have, the more stable and strong you will be.

The ultimate belief, from which all other beliefs stem, is your belief in God. A belief in an ultimate Creator and Sustainer of life is the nucleus to success.

It is through this ultimate belief that you obtain unshakable faith. The main substance that was missing from my life at the time of my Bermuda breakthrough, was a personal relationship with God. I knew I needed to spend time getting to know God again. I had enjoyed that spiritual closeness at one time, but, through my own excuses, I no longer did. I did not know His power because I wasn't spending time with Him. I did not have unshakable faith because I didn't spend time with the One who imparts faith. I made a commitment that day to spend an hour with God every day. I would pray, meditate over the Bible, and write down what He was showing me to do. It changed my life!

I felt so empowered through this decision of spending one hour with God every day! I knew my life would be an exciting, adventurous road, and most important, that it would have an eternal influence.

I think the reason why it was so easy for me to make this commitment to God was because of my background. I had, in the past, experienced firsthand the power that comes from a personal relationship with the living God.

# My Personal Testimony

I had the good fortune of being raised in a Bible-teaching home. I was taught at a young age about the love of God and the plan He had for my life.

My mom lived out her faith in every aspect of her life. I saw her walk her talk every day. I thought that because she was a Godly woman that I, too, would be shined upon by God and be accepted into His Kingdom through her faith. But, one Saturday afternoon, as I sat next to a beautiful lake—through a complete stranger—I found that I was wrong!

When I was 15 years old, I went to a praise and worship service at a non-denominational church. After the service I went for a walk along the surrounding lake. It was a beautiful day. Not long into my walk, a young man came up to me and started talking about the good news of the Gospel. He told me that history validates the person whose name is Jesus of Nazareth who came to earth, lived a perfect life, died by crucifixion, and rose from the dead. He told me that Jesus was the perfect sacrifice, the Redeemer, the Messiah, who "washed away the sins of the world" for every person who believes.

Well, I knew all this. I began to tell this total stranger that I had a mother who was a woman of faith and I knew God through her. He looked at me inquisitively and said, "We are all imperfect human beings—individual sinners—who are separated from a holy and perfect God. We each, individually, need to call on the Savior."

Something came over me that made me really listen, and somehow I understood the message that this guy was teaching. I knew I had to accept this truth with my own heart, and my own mind. I had been accepting it through my mom, but on that day, I believe God was asking me, as an individual, if I were willing to accept His great sacrifice and Him as my personal Savior.

So, right there on the bank of the lake, I accepted Jesus as my personal Savior with my own heart and mind. It was overwhelming! I never knew of such peace, joy, and unconditional love.

I was consumed with pure love!

Fifteen years later the same voice was calling me back to Him. With the same childlike voice, I answered, "I'm here Lord, and I love you."

I realized on that day that I have complete access to God and all His power... and so do you.

Do you hear Him calling your name and drawing you nearer to Him too? You don't have to get yourself cleaned up, dressed up, and fixed up, in order to have a personal relationship with Him. You just have to come to Him—just the way you are right now. He does the rest. You have to put your faith in the One who breathed you into existence. And when you do have a personal relationship with Him, you will be amazed at the power of your faith. It is your faith that will conquer all fear.

# Know Who You Are And Whose You Are

Creating a powerful belief system begins with *knowing who* you are; it is completed by *knowing whose* you are. The blending of the two disciplines of psychology and spirituality is your winning combination to conquering your fear and cultivating unshakable faith.

In this section of the book you will take an introspective look at yourself, your values, and your beliefs. Take the time to do the exercises and write all over the pages. This is your personal workbook to help you along your journey to self-discovery!

*"To see what is in front on one's nose requires a constant struggle."*

—George Orwell

*Chapter 5*

# Discovering Who You Are... and Finding the Courage To Be That Person!

When you know who you are, you can build on where you want to go. Knowing who you are and what you value creates a powerful foundation that will give you incredible focus and strength during challenging times.

You know who you are when you can answer the following questions:

> 1. *What is my personality style?*
>
> 2. *What are my natural talents?*
>
> 3. *What are my leading values?*
>
> 4. *What is my purpose?*
>
> 5. *What do I really want?*

## Question 1: What is my personality style?

According to behavioral psychologists, there are four different personality styles. While every human being will have some traits from all four styles, one dominant style will emerge, influencing how you make decisions, handle rejection, deal with a challenge, relate to people, and bring out the best in you and others. This dominant personality style comes out most strongly under stress or pressure.

# The Four Personality Styles

I've listed four animals below. They represent each of the four personality styles. Without even knowing the details about which personality style each animal represents, choose which one you believe describes you the best.

**Activity #1:** Which of the four animals do you best relate to? Which one describes you the best?

| | |
|---|---|
| *Panther* | *Dolphin* |
| *Peacock* | *Owl* |

The animal that describes me the best is the: _____.

The other animal that describes me is the:_____.

The animal that describes me least is the _____.

Now, let's see how well you did. Here are the descriptions of each of the animals.

## Panther

Those with the panther personality are natural born leaders. They are great visionaries. They excel at seeing the big picture and putting together a grand function or idea. Panthers are focused and decisive. They are driven and goal-oriented. They are most often quick to make decisions, and they don't want a lot of information to muddle or confuse that decision. They are bottom-line thinkers and quick decision-makers. Panthers are people-oriented, but they occasionally lose patience with others and their differing opinions.

Panthers often act before thinking things through, which can cause important details to fall through the cracks. They are so goal-oriented and focused on the big picture that they can hurt the feelings of family or colleagues. They are often too bossy and don't listen carefully enough.

Panthers may need help with keeping balance in their lives because they are so driven. They do not like to waste time nor have their time wasted by others. They are disciplined people and love to work hard and accomplish a lot.

The panther's greatest value is **productivity**.

## Peacock

Those with the peacock personality are natural socialites. They meet people easily. They love to have fun and create a happy environment.

Peacocks relish making things a big event. They are the life of the party and need socializing and working as a group. Most peacocks are comfortable being the center of attention. They are people-focused and welcome commotion. They handle chaos well and look at it as an adventure.

Peacocks are not great listeners. They need to work on letting others tell their story. They can be disorganized and misplace items, due to their inability to focus on details. Peacocks are willing and eager to learn new skills and enjoy challenges and risk-taking.

The peacock's greatest value is **fun**.

## Dolphin

Those with the dolphin personality are natural givers. They are great listeners and loyal friends. They ask questions and love to find out about their clients, friends, and family. Dolphins value being a part of a team. They are very loyal and will stay in a situation forever if possible, which sometimes is too long. Because dolphins are service-minded people. Their greatest challenge is in not ministering to themselves. They can become resentful because they often don't get their needs met.

They do not like change but do tolerate it if it means being helpful to the team. They are slow to make decisions and stick with them when they do finally make them. Dolphins are easy-going, easy to work with, and easy to train.

The Dolphin's greatest value is **relationships**.

## Owl

Those with the owl personality pay keen attention to detail. They prefer tasks over people and enjoy working or playing alone. They are incredibly observant and will notice (and remember) the little things. Owls need time to think about decisions. They like a lot of information. They are independent thinkers and prefer behind-the-scenes tasks. They don't speak a lot, but when they do speak, they are very wise. Owls may cause hurt feelings because they don't share their feelings easily. They are more introverted with their ideas and thoughts. They can lose an opportunity because they take too long make a decision, or they don't share their thoughts on a decision. They do not like change and don't handle change well. Owls are very detail- oriented.

The owl's greatest value is **security**.

**Activity #2:** Circle the words in this list that you think best describe you.

> *motivator, thorough, leader, entertainer, sequential, giver, risk-taker, colorful, detail-oriented, follower, focused, exciting, attention to detail, big thinker, quick-witted, outspoken, fun, peace-maker, analytical, giver, insightful, listener, slow to change, adventurous, methodical, introspective, orderly.*

Out of the words you circled, write the top five words that best describe you on the lines below.

_____        _____

_____        _____

_____

## Panther

*motivator*

*leader*

*risk-taker*

*focused*

*big thinker*

*outspoken*

*adventurous*

## Peacock

*motivator*

*entertainer*

*colorful*

*exciting*

*quick-witted*

*fun*

*adventurous*

## Dolphin

*peace-maker*

*giver*

*follower*

*insightful*

*listener*

*slow to change*

*introspective*

## Owl

*thorough*

*detail oriented*

*sequential*

*attention to detail*

*analytical*

*methodical*

*orderly*

Great pride and freedom come from knowing who you are and that you were not meant to have all strengths. Living authentically to your personality style will free you to be yourself and allow you to realize how much all of us need each other. Picture a puzzle with hundreds of individual pieces that make up the beautiful, finished product. Each puzzle piece has a protruding part and a recessed part. It is the same with talents and natural gifts. You have something to offer with your gifts, but you also have limitations and voids, which you needs others to provide in order to complete the finished product.

When you accept the fact that we all have different personality styles, you see the beauty of God's plan for balance in this world. The problem comes when we are not true to ourselves and try to be someone we are not!

# Natural Talents and Abilities

## Question 2: What are my natural talents?

You have been equipped with all you need to make your life work. Look to your natural inborn talents to guide you in your purpose. You know those things you do so well that you don't even have to think about it. It is those abilities that come naturally to you which are your natural talents.

**Activity #3:** Write six one-word positives that best describe you.

_____     _____

_____     _____

_____     _____

Now ask your spouse, colleague, or children to identify what they see are your natural abilities using one-word positives. Do they match? Did they surprise you?

_____     _____

_____     _____

_____     _____

# Core Values

## Question 3: What are my leading values?

We all have core values that motivate our behaviors in a powerful way. These core values come from our internal personality style and our external life experiences. These leading core values cause us to react a certain way, say yes to particular choices, and even affect our emotions, decisions, and happiness.

When you are aware of your core values and you do things in your life to fulfill them, you feel great! Have you ever been in the middle of a very challenging project and felt energized by it? Everything you did in the process was rewarding. By the same token, you've probably had a project that drained you. You just went through the motions and couldn't wait for it to be over. It is when your core values are being fulfilled that you are energized and at your peak performance.

**Activity #4:** Answer the following questions as honestly as you can.

What are the three most important things in your life?

_____        _____

_____

What was the most recent thing you've done to show that you value what you listed at number one? If you put family at the top of your list, but you are too busy with work commitments, to be with your family, then you will be miserable! You may question why you are unhappy. You will find the reason when you answer these two questions: What are your highest values? And, do you spend time valuing those values daily with your actions, thoughts and time? If your highest value is God and you are not spending time with Him in prayer and meditation, then you will be miserable! If your highest value is health and you are not spending enough time working out, then you feel unfulfilled! Your time, efforts, thought, and energies must be spent on your highest values in order to create a life you love.

**Activity #5:** Whom do you really admire? Name three people— living or dead, famous or not—as the people you most look up to. Don't think too much. Just write the three that come to mind first.

The three people I admire the most are:

_____        _____

_____

**Activity #6:** Write down why you admire those three people. What qualities or characteristics do they have that you value?

| Person's Name | Reason you admire him/her |
|---|---|
| _____ | _____ |
| _____ | _____ |
| _____ | _____ |

What you wrote is very reflective to what you value. People seem to admire those characteristics in others that best reflect their own core values.

This exercise helps you focus on **who you are** rather than **what you do**. It is important to know what you value, and what character qualities you value, so you know who you want to become along the way. You grow visualizing who you want to be and disciplining yourself to take the steps necessary to become that person.

When your goals (what you do) and your values (who you are) are congruent, you will have created your formula for lifelong motivation and fulfillment. You will be living in a life that you love!

At the end of a two-day retreat I gave on working to one's full potential, a lady approached me.

"I finally get it," she said. "I finally get why I'm so unhappy."

I was taken back. I looked at her with an inquisitive face and asked, "Tell me what you discovered."

*Mary's story:*

Mary had started a small advertising company seven years ago.

"When I first started my company I loved going to work," she began. "I would work on my business plan. I'd worked the numbers, set up appointments, write up and present proposals. I would fulfill the job or sub it out to a major company. I loved the behind-the-scenes, organizational, detailed work.

When I started to get a good number of clients, I began to hire staff. It was great at first. But, it didn't last long. You see, I was the boss in charge of these employees. I had to motivate them and hold weekly staff meetings. I hated doing all the people stuff. But I knew it was what I had to do to continue my company's success."

Mary had been managing her staff for the past three years and was just about burned out. You see, Mary is a "behind-the-scenes" kind of person. She enjoys all the paper-work, organization, and attention to detail. She prefers to work alone.

"People are fine, but not to be around all day and definitely not to work with and motivate daily," she explained.

We all have these core values that coincide with our personality style and life experiences. When we are able to live out these core values in our work and home environment, we are happy people. We are fulfilled. Life feels good.

Just like Mary, you need to discover what you value along with your personality style. Does your job reflect your values and style? Work can be an exhausting, tortuous, even downright unhealthy activity when it doesn't correlate with your personality style and core values. When you become aware of your personality style and core values, and put them in alignment, you will create the formula for lifelong motivation.

## Question 4: What is my purpose?

People often come to me after my seminar and ask how they can find their purpose and know they are fulfilling it. I always reply that they must realize they already know what their unique purpose is. Purpose is not something you need to search for.

Purpose wells up from your very being. Your purpose in life has always been with you. It was written on your soul before time. All of your life you have been given circumstances, challenges, hurts, and successes to help you fulfill your life purpose. It will coincide with your personality and core values. It will reflect your childhood hurts and experiences.

**Activity # 7:** One of the exercises you can do to discover this purpose is to think back when you were a child and had hours of free time to play make believe.

What did you do with those hours of free time? What was the one thing you loved to do so much, that you would even miss a meal for? Remember, your mom calling you in for dinner and you would yell back, "Just five more minutes, Mom!" For me, it was playing school. I would line up all my "students" in rows or in groups, call the roll, explain the lesson, and teach, teach, teach until my mom would call me for dinner.

Your childhood play is very revealing to what your purpose is.

*My favorite activity as a child was: _____*

_____.

When our family went on vacation a few years ago, I unpacked all our clothes and shoes in the single closet provided in the hotel room. My three-year-old son, Beau, started playing with all the different shoes in the closet. When I went back to check on him a few minutes later, he had designed a rainbow! He put all the different-sized shoes in an arch—asymmetrically! One baby shoe on the right side, one baby shoe on the left side. One high- healed shoe above it on the right side, its match on the left! His natural gifts that I witnessed in his youth still evident today. It is amazing to see the correlation between life purpose and childhood play.

Another way to discover your unique purpose is to look back at your childhood hurts. There is power in pain. There is power in your childhood hurts if they are dealt with and forgiven. Imagine how your childhood pain could be used for ultimate good by taking a childhood hurt, dealing with it, forgiving it, and using it to better relate to others who may be going through what you did. Nobody knows how to help another person better than the one who went through it and has successfully coped and survived! The truth about your childhood hurts is that if you choose not to deal with them; then they deal with you. The pain comes out in your attitude, your behavior, even in the choices you make for yourself. You can either numb yourself, or allow it to be your motivation to do some good.

God promises us that He will use bad circumstances for ultimate good. What pain have you experienced in your past that you don't want to deal with or have not forgiven? I urge you to reconsider. Your decision to forgive it, deal with it, and then share it could bring you your greatest fulfillment. Some of the most powerful messengers are those who are willing to share their past pain. Every one of us has had our share.

There is no such thing as a perfect family or perfect parents. So get over the lie that you are the only one who had to go through that pain. The people in your childhood who loved you (and even those who refused to love you) and the pain in your childhood all shaped the person you are today. They are all a part of your life purpose. You can allow your pain to motivate you to speak out and work for ultimate good. What a gift you have to give when you are willing to look at your pain as a possibility for good! The joys and pains of your childhood create in you a strong understanding and commitment to God's plan for your life.

*Joe's story:*

Joe was physically abused in his childhood. He lived most of his adult life in a constant state of anger. He didn't trust anyone and habitually criticized others. He always had to be in control, which was his way of dealing with the childhood pain of not having control.

But Joe knew he needed help. He invited a couple from a local church to come over to his house one night. When they arrived ten minutes late, however, he cursed at them and threw them out! Can you believe that?

Well, that couple didn't give up. Several visits later Joe chose to bring those childhood hurts to the present consciously (remember he had already brought them to the present subconsciously). Over the next several months Joe dealt with his past hurts and learned to forgive them. Today he works as a social worker, providing a listening ear to prison inmates who have been abused in their childhood.

Joe talks about the power and contentment he feels now. Living out his unique purpose every day has brought him a fulfilling life.

There's power—so much power—in childhood hurts that are brought to the present, dealt with, forgiven... and then used to help others.

Everyone has childhood hurts and unmet needs. Most are not as dramatic as Joe's. But, all childhood hurts are part of the most important pieces in preparing you for your life's purpose. Listen to yourself. Listen to God's voice guiding you in the plan He has created for you. A truly fulfilling life is one of purpose. When you are living your purpose, your life will be full of peace, passion, and pure joy. Even in the heat of negative circumstances, your life's purpose will carry you past pain, rejection, frustration, and difficulty. As one colleague of mine, Liz Curtis Higgs, says, "Turn down the noise and listen to the One who made you."

*"The problems of people's pasts impact them in one of two ways: They experience either a breakdown or a breakthrough."*

*—John C. Maxwell*

# Creating A Life You Really Love

## Question 5: What do I really want?

Tim, a successful defense attorney, was bored with his job. He longed to leave his practice and to start a computer consulting business. His real passion was tinkering around on his computer, spending hours after work and on the weekend learning everything he could about computers.

A prestigious law firm in Washington offered Tim a job. It was a good offer, a safe way for Tim to make a change. And, after all, law was what Tim new, what he went through seven years of school to do, what his parents always told him he'd be great at.

So, Tim and his wife, Gail, put their house on the market and flew out to Washington to find a house there. Everything seemed to be rolling along the way it was supposed to. Safe. Practical. Predictable.

And then, one afternoon as they were househunting, Gail looked at Tim and said, "Do you really want to move here? Do you really want to do the same thing you've done for so long?"

After a long silence, during which Tim finally thought about what he really wanted, he whispered, "No. I don't." he shared with Gail his dream of opening his own consulting business, and she encouraged him to pursue it.

Tim said he had to fight the practical bug every step of the way. Six months into his consulting business he had more clients than planned, and was doing better than if he had stayed with his safe job, had chosen the practical thing to do. Best of all, he was doing what he really wanted to do.

It seems odd that grown people would not know what they want and often don't hold the power to act on their dreams. Yet, it is very common. Kids, on the other hand seem to know exactly what they want. Why? One reason is that they have the time to daydream, fantasize, think. Adults don't take the time to daydream or think about what they would really love to do.

If you haven't asked yourself lately what you want, then you probably don't know the answer. You are either living out someone else's dreams for you or you are settling for what's simply good when you could have what is the best. Either leads to an unfulfilled life, to feelings of resentment, to inevitably asking the question, "Is this all there is?"

Have you ever taken the time to think about what your dream life would be like? What job would you have? What time would you get up most mornings? Who would be in your life? What would your day look like? How would you be spending your time?

I have kept a dream book for over twenty-one years. In this book I write down (and even draw pictures) of what my dream life would look like. The most amazing part about this dream book has been watching myself grow into my dreams. I'll look back at my dreams of five years ago and think, "Gosh, I did that—no problem." So many of the things I've written down have come to be!

There is so much power in knowing what you want. Clarity gives you power. When you know what you want, and you begin acting on those wants (even in very small ways), every day of your life looks more exciting. If you were to look back at your life so far, you would see unfolding miracles that made your life events. You were provided with what you needed when you needed it, usually not before. Every event that happens in your life is moving you a little closer to your destination. There is a process going on in your life.

If it's true that God gives you the desires of your heart, then it is imperative that you know your desires and have the courage to communicate them. It is God who places the desires of your life in your heart. You will begin the process of creating them by first taking the time to realize and communicate them.

When you do achieve what you want, don't forget that you got what you wanted. In my case, I always wanted to be a mother. Now, as a mother of three, I find that the demands can be so overwhelming I lose sight of the fact that I have exactly what I wanted. I wanted to have kids, a family, a house, even a mini-van!

Now I make sure I do something every day with my kids that we enjoy doing so I don't lose sight of the fact that I got what I wanted.

Don't get so bogged down with the responsibility of your goal that you forget the fact that it is what you wanted!

Some of you are still not clear on what you want. I see it every day in working with people. They either don't say what they really want or they just don't know. Knowing is an important part of this whole process. Be crystal clear about what it is you want. This clarity brings power. You will be amazed at how much this simple habit will eliminate your fear and begin to attract opportunity to you.

You can be sure you are working toward your right goals if you answer yes to these questions: Do you have your goals (dreams) written down? Do you think about them often, and do you back up your dreams, desires and goals with action (even small efforts)?

## Activity #8:

Write down your goal, using as much detail as possible.

_____

Make a list of action steps you need to take to begin the process of achieving that goal.

_____

_____

_____

Make a list of ten people who will help you achieve this goal.

_____     _____

_____     _____

_____     _____

_____     _____

_____     _____

When you know what you want, you begin to attract people, opportunity, and relationships that help you achieve your dream. Pull, don't push. Attract people and opportunity to you by knowing who you are, celebrating your uniqueness, and obeying that unique calling God has for you.

## Activity #9:

The activity that brings me the most joy is

_____

I feel most alive when I am

_____

One way I could put this activity in my life more is

_____

Decide where you want to be in ten years. twenty years. fifty years. ten years:

_____

_____

twenty years:

_____

_____

fifty years:

_____

_____

Get in the habit of continually asking yourself such questions as "Are my actions in alignment with my beliefs?" "Is this how I want to react?" "Is this how I choose to handle this?" These questions are essential to implementing any change, because they put you in control. Most people don't even think about how they are behaving, let alone ask these questions of themselves. When you are aware of what you are doing or how you are choosing to react to the challenges of your life, you will control your ultimate success and who you become along the way.

Thinking and asking yourself questions demands silence, stillness, contemplation. Since we are a society of fast-paced action, we often get numb to what's going on around us and our feelings about it. In this state of numbness you cannot be aware of your thoughts or your behavior. Be different. Ask yourself questions. Know what you want, write it down and think (dream) about it. You will be surprised at what happens and will enjoy the results!

## Summary

I believe each of us already has within us all that we need to make our lives work. The reality is, our lives are an intricately woven tapestry of unique gifts, talents, temperaments, personality styles, and even childhood hurts.

These aspects work together, creating the framework for personal and professional success. Whatever you have that is unique and different forms your power. The things about you that make you feel a little uncomfortable are the very things that contain treasures that will lead you to your purpose and a fulfilled life. What gift came from your childhood that you may have dismissed? Which unique talent, passion or interest do you contain that you shun or disregard? Give in to the artist, the musician, the actress, the parent, or the business professional you always dreamed of being, and intuitively know you are.

Figure out a way to bring those magnificent gifts and experiences out. Think about them often. Dream about them often. Continue to ask yourself questions. You will discover an unceasing treasure that is part of your success equation. My challenge to you, the reader, is to look at yourself and others and see the rarity; celebrate that uniqueness and have the courage to be yourself.

*"It's a funny thing about life: If you refuse to accept anything but the best, you very often get it."*
—W. Somerset Maugham

# Chapter 6
# Knowing Whose You Are

Albert Camus, a famous author and philosopher, once applied names to the previous centuries. He named the seventeenth century as the century of math. The eighteenth was the century of physical. The nineteenth was the century of biology. Then, he shocked the public by naming the twentieth century the century of fear. Mr. Camus explained his reasons were evident in the fact that never before has their been such an overwhelming, massive use of tranquilizers.

In 1947 another philosopher and poet, W.H. Auden, called our time, "the age of anxiety."

What I noticed about these two reports is how recent the strong hold of fear is. From Biblical times all the way to the beginning of our great nation, fear did not have the domineering control that it does now. Anxiety was not a major concern. Worry and stress were not life-threatening problems like they are today.

How were our ancestors able to handle their circumstances without fear and anxiety consuming their very beings? What was their secret to handling famine, war, flooding, disease, and death, (let alone everyday life challenges)?

The greatest difference between our ancestors and us is they knew whose they were. God ruled their universe. Their strong faith and belief in God guided their lives.

Read the biographies of our forefathers and you will see a people of great faith in God. Read the Old Testament stories and see how the Jewish people handled and dealt with anxiety. Their faith out-weighed their fear. They were not controlled by their fears, worry, or anxiety because of their tremendous faith. Faith in God, not self, was the prevalent way of life.

With the advent of the Renaissance and humanism, a dramatic shift took place in the way society viewed God and man. The great goal of humanism, ushered in through the Renaissance, was to master one's own environment, to be one's own god, to be independent and self-sufficient.

Humanism shouts, "You don't need anybody." "You don't need God." The message is clear. This belief says you have the power to raise your consciousness and create your own success apart from God. With the birth of humanism, we began to lose our knowledge of who God is and what our place is in Him. When this happens, the whole world becomes embroiled in lack of trust, extreme competition, lack of faith, anxiety, tremendous fear and other self-defeating conditions.

It's no surprise that we have more people on tranquilizers than ever before in our history! We now have sayings like, "It's a dog-eat-dog world." "Look out for number one." "You only live once." "Eat, drink, and be merry, for today may be your last." Without much thought, we accept this view as thew ay of life. We have taken God and prayer out of our public sector and wonder why our nation is consumed with fear and called the age of anxiety and the century of fear.

Darrell Scott, the father of Rachel Scott, a victim of the Columbine High School shootings in Littleton, Colorado, was invited to address the House Judiciary Committee several weeks after his daughter was murdered by two school mates. What he said to our national leaders during this special session of Congress was painfully truthful.

*"We all contain the seeds of kindness or the seeds of violence," he began. "The first recorded act of violence was when*

*Cain slew his brother Abel out in the field. The villain was not the club he used. Neither was it the NCA, the National Club Association. The true killer was Cain, and the reason for the murder could only be found in Cain's heart.*

*"I am not here to represent or defend the NRA because I don't believe that they are responsible for my daughter Rachel's death. I am here today to declare that Columbine was not just a tragedy—it was a spiritual event that should be forcing us to look at where the real blame lies! Much of the blame lies here in this room. Much of the blame lies behind the pointing fingers of the accusers themselves.*

*"Men and women are three-part beings. We all consist of body, soul, and spirit. When we refuse to acknowledge a third part of our makeup, we create a void that allows evil, prejudice, and hatred to rush in and wreak havoc. Eric and Dylan would not have been stopped by metal detectors. No amount of gun laws can stop someone who spends months planning this type of massacre. The real villain lies within our own hearts. We do not need more religion. What we need is a change of heart and a humble acknowledgment that this nation was founded on the principle of simple trust in God!*

*"As my son Craig lay under that table in the school library and watched his two friends murdered before his very eyes, he did not hesitate to pray in school. I defy any law or politician to deny him that right! I challenge every young person in America, and around the world, to realize that on April 20, 1999, at Columbine High School, prayer was brought back to our schools."*

He closed with an emotional poem he wrote to express his feelings:

*"Your laws ignore our deepest needs, your words are empty air. You've stripped away our heritage, you've outlawed simple prayer. Now gunshots fill our classrooms, and precious children die.*

*You seek for answers everywhere, and ask the question "Why?"*
*You regulate restrictive laws, through legislative creed,*
*And yet you fail to understand, that God is what we need!"*

Where was God when the Columbine shootings were taking place at that public high school? The answer is simple. "He wasn't invited."

Since 1963, God and prayer have been taken out of our nations public school. This nation has chosen not to invite God into the school sector of a child's life.

And the cold truth is, if you take prayer and God out of school, then millions of American children are not being told about Him, don't know Him, and don't know whose they are in Him.

This was never the way our founding fathers intended it to be. Spiritual influences were present within our educational systems for all of our nation's history. Many of our major colleges began as theological seminaries. This is a historical fact.

Our ancestors had incredible faith in God and each other. They knew whose they were and they drew great strength from their faith. God wants us to depend on Him for our strength. He promises to equip and sustain us to the highest power—His power!

Knowing whose you are means acknowledging there is a sovereign God who loves you, knows you, has a purpose for you, will sustain you, and wants a personal relationship with you. God tells those who believe in Him that they are royalty. He calls believers, "My beloved." When you view yourself in this way, you will begin behaving like royalty and the beloved. Conversely, when you take away God and His perimeters for a healthy, happy life, you take away the very foundation of peace, power, and a life void of fear, worry, anxiety, and depression.

What you believe about yourself attracts opportunity to you. It will attract the right people to you and is a large part of creating your success.

# *The Princess*

When I was a girl, our family would often visit some special friends. These friends had a daughter named Michelle, whom everyone (including my parents) affectionately referred to as "Princess." Since there could only be one princess, I was referred to as "Duchess." It may sound silly, but I can still remember how much I hated that nickname, because it made me feel less important.

Although I never saw myself as second place, to a seven-year-old, being a duchess was definitely second place. Despite how I felt, I silently kept my feelings buried within me. Yet they must have shown.

One day, nearly fifteen years later, a package arrived in the mail for me. It was from the "princess's" mother. I tore open the packaging to discover a glittery box tied in red velvet ribbon. My eyes lit up as I saw what was in the box: a tiny, golden Cinderella carriage and a note that read, "You were always a princess to me."

How do you see yourself? When you look at your reflection, what and who do you see? Even if you weren't fortunate enough to have people around you in your youth who believed in you, you can still take comfort in knowing that God thinks everything of you. He loved you enough to breathe life into you. He loved you enough to equip you with all you need to make your life work. He loved you enough to sustain you through the most difficult time. He loved you enough to send His Son as an atonement for sin. God is desperately in love with you! He is pursuing you even as you read this book.

Look back through your life and you will see the evidence of a mighty God who loves you in a mighty way. Your understanding of God's perception of you defines your reality and will be the source of your power and strength.

When you know whose you are and that you have a role to play in His sovereign plan, you will experience peace that surpasses all understanding and gain great confidence that comes from the Source of confidence.

# Our Ancestors' Guiding Principles

Our ancestors had four principles in place, which empowered them with nourishment in times of famine, courage in times of disease, and strength in times of war. In the research I did for this book, I witnessed the same principles lived out in modern-day success stories. The four principles are:

*Live your life in faith.*

*Know that God has a plan for you.*

*Be a person of prayer.*

*Have an eternal focus.*

## 1. Live Your Life in Faith

The opposite of fear is faith. It is through faith that you will banish fear, anxiety, procrastination, and all the other symptoms fear creates.

Faith is like a multivitamin on steroids! It is faith that fosters hope, courage, boldness, and conviction. Many books seek to motivate you to feel your fears and do what needs to be done anyway. But they don't tell you how. So, this plan may work... for a while. But, when you are faced with more fear, this approach fails you because it only deals with your thoughts and not your beliefs behind those thoughts. The good news that Conquer Fear brings you is the "how" to feel the fear and move ahead anyway, and that is by cultivating your faith. Walk into your fear with faith in your Creator, in your talents, and the ultimate, sovereign plan He has created for you. Over 360 times, the Scriptures say, "Fear not!" The Bible never said "No Fear!" as many people have changed its wording to be. Fear is very real, and it isn't going away. It is in finding your faith that you will be able to befriend your fear and then fear not. You have control over your fear. When you know whose you are and believe you are called to accomplish a specific and unique purpose, your faith will be all you need to conquer your fear and complete the work intended for you.

## Finding Your Faith

What is faith? Webster's definition of faith is "belief, trust, or reliance." The Apostle Paul's definition is "Faith is the assurance of things hoped for and the conviction of things not seen." Do you have the assurance of things hoped for, and a strong conviction that, even though you can't see them, they exist and will happen?

When you cultivate your faith—faith in your Creator, faith in yourself, faith in your purpose and mission—you will be an unstoppable, powerful force!

The headline read, "Faith is more important than food." That was the conclusion of a recent medical report, which studied the correlation between stress and ulcers. The report cited that ulcers were by-products of anxiety, worry, and fear. It went on to discuss how faith is a cure for a patient suffering from an ulcer. Even the medical community recognizes the power of faith. To an ulcer patient writhing in pain, faith is more important than food.

Days after I read the ulcer report, that statement remained with me. "Faith is more important than food." I realized this is true for healthy people as well. It applies to parents doing all they can to raise healthy, happy kids. It applies to spouses trying hard to keep their marriage alive or even keeping it together. Faith applies to professionals working hard to make a sale. The most important ingredient for an ulcer patient is the same for all people. That ingredient is faith.

Your efforts and hard work will create results. Your efforts and hard work motivated by faith will produce peace in those results. The person who lacks faith can never experience true freedom and happiness.

Why? Because faith creates belief, confidence, courage and focus—the very qualities attributed to creating and maintaining success.

The great truth about faith is that you already have access to it. Faith is a gift from God, your Creator. But many live today without cultivating their gift of faith and never experience the power of cultivating its power.

Faith is like a muscle. It needs to be used, developed, and exercised in order to be most effective. Faith acts! The more you use your faith the stronger and stronger it becomes.

You may be asking, "How do I begin to use this gift of faith and witness its great power?"

## Faith Takes A Relationship

If I were to describe what it takes to cultivate faith, I would answer with one simple sentence: "Faith takes a relationship with God." The birth of this kind of faith comes about by acknowledging that a sovereign God exists who created you for a distinct purpose and through a relationship with Him, you will live out great things. God is glorified when He does great things through His people. He wants you to succeed!

Acknowledging His existence—let alone a personal relationship with Him—may be difficult for you because, if you're like most people, you cannot describe your faith or what God means to you. And anything that we can not describe we have trouble believing in.

I realized this firsthand in doing research for this book. I gave the following question to people of different ages and genders and was shocked at some of their answers. Answer the following two questions and see what you come up with:

When I say the word "flower," what picture comes to your mind? Visualize a flower. Write down and describe what you see.

_____

_____

Some of you may have seen a simple red rose, or a bouquet of yellow daisies. Some of you are more elaborate and you visualized a garden filled with every flower imaginable! That is your association with flowers. You can easily create the vision in your mind.

Now, when I say the words "God the Father," what picture comes to your mind? Visualize God the Father. Describe what you see:

_____

_____

Not as easy is it? Some of you may have seen a bright light or an older gray-haired man sitting on a throne. Still others may see a judgmental image counting the flaws of mere mortals.

These are your various associations with your Creator. The problem arises when your belief system creates a negative image of who God really is. Millions of people miss out on their gift of faith, or they never experience its full power in their lives, because they have a negative image of God. If you have a negative image or a negative belief about God, you will never be able to experience ALL the great blessings that come from being in a personal relationship with Him. And because of this, you are missing a link for creating success. That link is FAITH through a relationship with the living, loving God.

Your relationship with God is dramatically related to your relationship with fear. Without a vision of a loving, sovereign, omnipotent God, you will continue to live your life by just getting by, doing okay, hanging in there, and living day to day. But, that was never God's intention for you!

God created you to be in communion with Him. You are the only part of creation that was created in His image. You are the only creature created with a soul. Therefore, you are the only part of creation specifically designed to be in a relationship with Him.

God has placed a desire in every human being that only He can fulfill. (He did that to ensure His people would search for Him.) And because of this, people desperately search for a way to fill this desire. They look to other people, sex, the pursuit of money, fame, achievement, crystals, food, legalism, success, intelligence, drugs, marriage, parenthood, and many other ways to fill this desire, but none of them work. Even though they may have created success, accomplished their goals, so many people say, "Is this all there is?"

People desperately want God encounters. And the great truth is God desperately wants people encounters. He will meet you if you search for Him. Even if you are a professed atheist or agnostic, you can call out to the God who breathed life into you and say, "I don't think You exist. But, if You do, show Yourself to me." God has promised He will show Himself to you and change your heart and your mind.

With a vision of a living, loving Father who longs for you to come to Him in prayer and tell Him your fears, you can live a life of courage and faith, completely void of worry and anxiety. You can be freed from worry today!

When you worry, you actually hurt God. The Bible says, "A worried heart is a wicked heart." Recognize worry and lack of faith for what it is: the sin of unbelief. God doesn't want you to worry. He wants you to heed His admonition, which is, "All things work for good to those who believe and are called to His purpose." BELIEVE! Having faith is showing your belief in God. Faith is the most dramatic form of love.

Your faith is at its fullest when you don't worry about your circumstance, but replace that worry with faith in God's possibilities in your circumstances. You can not be controlled by your fears when you replace worry with awaiting God's answer. Your overwhelming life can lead you to an overwhelming God.

What could God do in your life if you let Him? What amazing things could He accomplish through you if you willingly chose faith over fear?

# Childlike Faith

As I'm writing this, there's a knock at the door. I open it to a smiling face of my two-year-old neighbor, Matthew. He expects me to open the door, return his smile with a bigger one, and be completely welcomed.

And, that's what happened. The first time he knocked, and the second time, and the third time. By the fourth knock I let him in, gave him a piece of licorice, and asked him to come back later. No where in his two-year-old mind was the thought of getting rejected. He has total faith that he will be welcomed and accepted (even after four knocks!).

"That's it!" I thought to myself. That's the kind of faith God wants us to have. God wants us to have a childlike faith.

When Connor, my six-year-old, started having bad dreams at night, he showed me how childlike faith works. Before going to sleep he would insist on praying to God, asking Him for kind thoughts and good dreams. He really believed that by saying that prayer he—without a doubt—would be free from having a nightmare!

This kind of faith is what our ancestors had. They cultivated their faith by living it daily. They witnessed God's great power throughout their lives because they lived out their faith. They had such great faith because they knew God, had built a relationship with Him. When you begin to live your life in faith through a relationship with God, you will see His unique plan being worked out for you every day.

## 2. Know that God has a plan for you:

Our ancestors honored the character of God. They knew He had a distinct plan for them. They trusted in God's plan for their life. "In God we trust" was printed on the currency. The first amendment of the Constitution was created to ensure the government would not get involved or influence religious expression. They honored God's character and lived out their faith to the fullest.

They knew God is omnipotent and omniscient. And they drew great strength and power from this belief. God has never had to learn anything. His knowledge is full from eternity past, present, and future. His knowledge is limitless.

God is sovereign. He has an ultimate plan. He has created you, equipped you, and positioned you to be a part of that great plan.

The problem arises today when our view of God is too small. We have lost our reverence of who God is. We have reduced God to TV programs, Sunday morning services, to nothing at all. Many have reduced God and His power and elevated themselves and what they can do individually.

I know of people who say, "I manifested that" when something good happens to them. Like the Renaissance man, they want to be self-sufficient and take care of themselves and then be deserving of all the glory. This is the popular belief of our culture today. In fact, there is a book, which has been read by millions of people, translated into twenty-four languages and was on the New York Times best seller's list for ninety-one weeks about this very belief.

The book is called Conversations with God. The core message is that there is no one God, but that we are all gods and can do all things on our own. The book reads, "Highly evolved cultures of the universe are clear that there is no separation between themselves and God."

One of the main reasons there is so much fear in people's lives today is because they see no separation and no difference between a holy God and themselves. They believe they are God. Many religions teach that mankind needs to establish a higher consciousness to commune with God—and ultimately become God. They believe if they meditate enough they will create Christ-consciousness and be one with God.

This is the primary reason I am so attracted to Christianity. It is the only religion where a holy God reaches down to mankind (not the other way around). It is the only religion that teaches mankind does nothing to deserve oneness with God. It is only in God's mercy and His very character that He reaches down to have a personal relationship with each one of us who choose to believe.

This doesn't mean you have no part in your relationship with God. Acknowledging your belief in Him—and your need for Him—is your component to connecting with God. You are a co-laborer with God. He uses your faith to instill His will. While God in the One manifesting His will and His miracles, it is your faith in Him that constitutes the power. Your part in connecting with God is your faith. And the stronger your faith, the more obvious are God's miracles.

Did you know that Jesus never performed any miracles in His home town? It is recorded in the book of Matthew that because Jesus found no faith in His land, He did no miracles there. Faith is our part in manifesting God's power. Faith is the criteria by which God works through His people. God's provision is as large as your faith.

All people, in the core of their being, have an instinctive need of God. They know their own efforts will at some point create despair. Fear will set in, a fear that consumes them, controls them, and eventually, slowly kills their faith.

Our ancestors' Biblical solution to cure fear, which is in direct opposition to the humanism view, is to humble yourself under the mighty hand of God and He will lift you up. You are created by God in His image, but not to be Him.

Humility means your life is not about you. It's about God's plan and how He can work miracles through you. Humility does not mean you don't attain success. It means that when you do attain success you know who made it all come about.

I recently heard a great story that talked about humility:

A successful businessman put a picture in his office of a turtle sitting on a fence post. When asked why, the man explained, "The turtle could not be up on that post unless someone put him there!" This picture reminded the businessman that in his success he should never forget who put him there. Now, that's true humility!

A good analogy of humility is the story of how the moon gets its light. The moon's light is empowered by the reflection of the sun's power. Humility is the glow within your life reflected from radiance from God.

The apostle Peter's Biblical solution to cure fear is to humble yourself under the mighty hand of God and He will lift you up.

William Beebe was a biologist, explorer, author, and a personal friend of Theodore Roosevelt. I read that he used to visit Roosevelt at his home near Oyster Bay, Long Island. He tells of a little game that they used to play together.

After an evening of talk, Roosevelt and Beebe would go outside onto the lawn surrounding the great house and search the sky until they found the faint spot of light beyond the lower left corner of the great square of Pegasus. One of them would recite: "That is the Spiral Galaxy in Andromeda. It is as large as the Milky Way. It is one of a hundred million galaxies. It consists of one hundred billion suns, each larger than our sun. And God made it all."

Then Roosevelt would grin at Beebe and say, "Now I think we know we are small enough and God is big enough. Let's go to bed!"

The people who know God's greatness, and their need of Him, are the people who live their life by faith—the kind of faith that can move mountains.

Paul tries to explain God in Romans and ends the chapter with, "Oh, the depths of God. How unsearchable are His ways" and "Who has known the mind of the Lord? Or who has been His counselor?" No person, with our human minds, can completely understand God and His ways. But, you can rest assured that His plan is in process even now while you read this book. There are no accidents. Every circumstance you have and every person you encounter is all part of His ultimate plan for your life.

When you know the character of God, you can be comforted in His power. You can find great joy and peace in the fact that He knows all about you—every little, deep, dark secret—and still loves you. He knows every detail about what's going on in your life and is positioning you right now in His ultimate plan for you. Nothing slips through the view of God.

I recently asked my three kids who they need to obey. They all chimed out, "We have to obey our father and our mother." (Such brilliant children!) Then I told them that one day they would be adults and would not have to obey us any more. When I asked them who they need to obey then, they were stumped. After a long pause, Beau jumped up and said, "We have to obey God!"

Anne Lamott, author of *Traveling Mercies* wrote, "Most of the people I know who have purpose, heart, balance, and joy are people of faith.

They follow a brighter light than the glimmer of their own candle."

There is a book in existence today which has withstood the test of time. It has been translated into every language known, has been read by millions across the globe and contains the very thoughts of God. Yes, it's the Bible. This book's core message is this: There is one God, and God created all things for a purpose. He is interested in you, cares for you, and wants a personal relationship with you for eternity. This book teaches you not to put your faith in yourself, but to anchor yourself in God, Himself.

Picture yourself in a boat—the boat of life. When you anchor your faith in yourself and at one point throw over your anchor, you destroy yourself. But when you anchor yourself in God and at some point throw over the anchor, He brings forth peace, assurance, and strength. How much more could you accomplish through Him?

When God calls us to rejoice, He is giving us the answer to conquering the three goal-killers: worry, anxiety, and fear. Conquer fear by cultivating your faith! Cultivate your faith by getting in a relationship with God. It will change your life. It will transform your thinking, empower you to conquer your fear, and give you courage to accomplish all you are meant to do.

Great faith begins with knowing God's character. But, knowledge without application is useless. Now, you can apply this knowledge, and watch it dramatically change your life for the better, through prayer.

## 3. Be a Person of Prayer

What do you want when you love someone? You want to spend time with them! That's why prayer is so important to God. He loves you and wants to spend time with you. He wants to know you love Him. Prayer, which is talking to God, is one of the ways to show that you love Him.

If you find that your life is too busy to spend quiet time with God, then you will never experience His great power.

As I mentioned earlier, after my Bermuda breakthrough, the one thing I did that created the most dramatic difference in my life was spending an hour with God every day. I knew that in order to get to know Him, I had to spend time with Him. This hour with God gives me a powerful focus and potent courage. I am different because of it. And I like the person I am turning into. I like the peace, confidence, and joy I have found. Developing my prayer life has made me a better person and it will do the same thing for you.

Are you exhausted with controlling your day and the people around you? Are you consumed with the fear of losing control and facing failure? When you decide to spend time with your Creator, listen to His plan for your life, and let Him empower you through it, you will find the cure to these ailments. You will walk into any situation with incredible courage—because you know you are not alone. You can rest in knowing that it doesn't matter if the outcome is an instant success or not because you know it is a part of the ultimate plan. And you are walking with the Creator of that plan.

One of the biggest misconceptions about prayer is that it is re-served for priests, pastors, or the "religious". This is a lie. Every person has access to God. There is no requirements to prayer. God desperately wants people-encounters. It is His way to show Himself, His great power, and build faith.

When you know somebody loves you, you'll give them anything you've got. Your money is open to them. Your schedule is open to them. It is the same way with God. When He knows you love Him, you will be the recipient of all that He has to give. When you decide to be committed to prayer, you will witness His great capacity for love and great power to manifest good in your life.

"The eye has not seen, ears have not heard all the good things that God has made ready for those who love Him." the apostle Paul reminds us about God.

For me it came down to this: "Am I willing to surrender to God's will for my life? Am I will to stop settling for my good plan of success, to ensure I was the recipient of God's best plan for success?"

It was through prayer and spending time with God that I discovered His plan for my life. The ironic thing is His plan fit my personality and true desires perfectly. I always thought that following God's plan for my life meant doing all the things I hated to do, making sacrifices, following rules, I would grudgingly obey. Not true! I couldn't have been more wrong! What I discovered is God takes your talents, desires, and abilities (which He gave you in the first place) and uses every one of them for this ultimate plan.

When you know God's plan for your life you take on a whole new perspective. Your whole existence exudes confidence, joy, direction, and peace!

If you don't believe it, it's because you haven't seen it. You haven't seen the awesome power of God at work in the lives of the people who love Him. I have seen it. I believe the power of prayer and God's sovereignty because I've seen it!

I've seen the power of faith in action through Charlotte's life. Charlotte is working with Stanford University to create the first train in the United States that runs above the ground by magnetic force. This "God-sized" project could not have transpired without continual prayer, faith, and communication with God.

Charlotte was coming to visit me for the weekend, her plane scheduled to arrive early Friday afternoon. "Don't pick me up until Friday night," she said. "I'm meeting with the president of a national bank to ask for his financial support in the project."

I couldn't believe she had gotten an appointment so quickly since she had just made the decision to come that same week. When I asked her about it she replied, "I don't have an appointment. But God is telling me to go ask this guy to be an investor, so I will go."

I picked Charlotte up in front of the company's corporate office at six-thirty that Friday evening. She had a huge smile on her face and another investor in her project. Amazing! She opened the car door and said, "God is good!"

I've seen marriages that were doomed to end in disaster and through prayer, become revitalized and renewed. I watched Theresa, wife of an alcoholic, get on her knees before a sovereign God and ask Him for healing and a changed heart in her husband. And it happened! After years of being gripped with alcoholism, her husband finally came before her and God and admitted his problem and need for healing. Together they have sought help and received it. Today they know their instantaneous change came directly from God's grace and their willingness to go to God for help, wisdom, strength, and healing.

I've seen the power of God move in my cousin's life when Tom got a job offer in Chicago, both he and his wife, Jennifer, knew God was calling them to this move. So, they took a leap of faith, put their house on the market and made plans for the transfer. However, months went by and their house did not sell.

They became discouraged as they realized they were going to have to leave their home in Florida unsold.

One morning, as they were preparing the Florida house to be left, Tom stopped in his tracks and said, "Let's pray one more time that God will provide a buyer by this weekend and we close before we move to Chicago." So, they asked. They had their family ask. They had their friends ask. "God, if it's your will, please provide a buyer for our home before we leave for Chicago." They asked. They asked in faith. They asked expecting an answer.

You have not, because you ask not. The apostle Paul reminds us of this truth. Most people don't know the magnitude of God and consequently make Him too small. So, they never ask. Or, they think it's selfish to ask for their own needs and desires.

Asking is one of the most important steps to creating success. Many sales people recite beautiful sales pitches and then never ask for the sale. Most married people complain about the shortcomings of their spouse, but never ask for what they need. If you get one thing out of this chapter, I hope it's that you will begin to ASK for what you want! Begin by asking God. The Bible tells us that God's position is one of outstretched hands, willing to give to the one who asks in faith! Can you imagine? The God of the universe wants to give to you. He wants to bless you. He wants to answer your prayers so His great power will be magnified. But you need first to ASK!

The reason we don't ask is because we really don't believe He will answer our prayer. We've tried it before and it didn't work. God doesn't meet our time frame, so we give up on praying to Him. The reasons God doesn't answer our prayer are because He knows it wouldn't be good for us or He wants to grow our faith.

### 1. He knows it wouldn't be in your best interest:

A two-year-old was watching his dad chop vegetables one afternoon. The little boy was mesmerized by the shiny silver blade as he saw the sun's light reflect off the knife. He squealed in delight and begged his daddy to let him have a turn with the "toy." Even though the little boy begged for a turn, of course his daddy would not let him have the knife. This father is like our Heavenly Father. He knows what would hurt you and only gives what would be good for you.

### 2. He wants to increase your faith:

God doesn't answer prayer in some instances because He knows the waiting will increase your faith. This was the case with my cousins, Tom and Jen. Their prayer for God to sell their house wasn't answered initially. So, they stopped praying and started packing until they felt called to pray one more time. It was then that God could do the imaginable, the unthinkable, the outrageous. Here's the end of the story . . .

That weekend, a couple who had looked at their house twice before called. They wanted to see it again. "This could be it!" Tom and Jen said to each other.

At the very same time this couple was looking at their house, a different couple drove up their driveway asking for directions to an open house that they had seen advertised in that morning's paper.

"This isn't the house advertised in the paper." Tom told them, "but it is for sale and you're welcome to come in and take a look anyway." By the end of that weekend Tom and Jen had two offers on their home!

The couple that made the best offer and bought the house said they had one stipulation: They needed to be moved in by the first of March, two days before the scheduled move to Chicago!

This true story shows the character of God. He wants to give to those who ask. He is looking for people of faith to show His great power. When you ask in faith, He will surprise you by pouring out a blessing above and beyond your expectations!

Prayer increases your faith so you can win a victory over your fear. When you are a person of prayer, you begin to operate your life through faith. Everything about you is different. You don't feel the need to push for success. You stand confidently in God's truth and attract success to you!

When you are a person of prayer, your definition of success begins to change. Fame, money, (sex, drugs, and rock and roll) begin to come into the light and take on a totally different shape to you. You begin to identify with things with eternal value and not with things of this world that pass away.

# An Eternal Focus

## 4. Maintain an Eternal Focus

Do you know what is the greatest structure ever built? This structure is the only apparatus that can be seen from the moon. Do you give up?

What is the name of the man who built this huge, most special piece? Surely he will have earned a lasting remembrance, for the impact he made on this world. Yet, if you're like me, you can't remember what his name is or what the structure is or where it is found. This massive structure is the Great Wall of China built by the designer, Qin Shi Hyang Di. You'd think we would remember him and his great structure forever. But we don't.

What about the most beautiful structure in the world? We would definitely remember the most beautiful structure of all time. Does that person's name come to mind? Probably not. Most people don't remember the person's name who built the Taj Mahal, the most beautiful design of all time. Most of us couldn't even remember the name of our maternal great-grandma.

The waves of time wash our name away, wash our efforts away, like the waves that run over your footprints in the sand and wash them away as though they were never there.

When I was a second-grade teacher, I created my own reading program. It was founded on the principle that all children can learn to read. When I proposed the program to our school's principle, Ellen Flynn, she was both supportive and excited about the possibilities. She told me I would have to get special permission from the school board before I could implement my ideas.

After reviewing the plan and making a visit to my classroom, the board supported it too. We were given a budget, special permission, and a classroom of wonderful kids. It was a huge success! Children were learning and loving it. Test scores went up and everyone was thrilled with the great reading program. Every child who went through my classroom became a reader. Other teachers were asking me to give workshops and seminars on this great program.

Then, after six years of teaching the program, Mark and I decided to start our family. Since we had always said I would stay home to raise our children, I resigned my position as a school teacher. "Not a problem," I thought to myself as I packed up all my books, learning supplies, and games, "surely another teacher will carry on my program and the success will continue."

A year later I visited the school with my new baby daughter, Auriana. After saying hello to all of my colleagues, I went to my old classroom eager to see how the new teacher applied my reading program. But when I walked in the classroom I didn't see a trace of it.

"They probably added so much new material to the program they had to move it to a bigger classroom," I thought to myself. But, to my chagrin that was not the case at all.

After looking everywhere for signs of my program, I finally asked one of the teachers.

"Oh, Lisa, we meant to start up the program again. But with budget cuts and classroom increases, we just couldn't find the time" was the dreaded response I got.

I finally found my reading program that day—in the storage room, all twenty boxes neatly stacked away and forgotten. I got in my car and cried all the way home.

"It's all totally forgotten!" I shouted.

That painful experience helped change my focus in life. It helped me realize that programs never last forever, ideas never last forever, and every person is replaceable.

All things on this earth pass away. All stars here on earth, whether it be rock stars, movie stars, sports stars or stars in the sky, are all shooting stars. They may be of great importance today. But they, like the footprints in the sand, will all be washed away and forgotten.

Just like our faith-filled ancestors, we can have an everlasting significance when we become concerned with what God is concerned with. I realized that the way to have an eternal influence is to be committed to the one thing on this earth that lives forever: another person's soul. Souls last forever! Souls are like stars of the kingdom. And those stars last for all time!

When I began to let God's passion be my passion, my focus changed. What I thought was of most importance began to change. I now had the complete equation for conquering fear and cultivating faith. This doesn't mean to stop pursuing, working, or creating—quite the opposite! It does mean that our pursuit, our work, and our creating takes on a different focus and a higher meaning.

This realization came full circle while writing this book. Nine months ago I had completed this writing project. As I read it and reread it to myself, I felt it was good. But something was missing. You see, I had written it from my research, experience, and head knowledge. I had not, however, included the heart research, experience, and knowledge. I had settled for my good, but not God's best. Even after I realized this, I was afraid to include the spiritual part because I wasn't sure it would "sell." God began to gently convict my motives and I went back to rewrite this book to include both the head and the heart knowledge for conquering fear.

I know the ultimate significance of my efforts and my work comes from being concerned with God's purpose, people's souls, and things that will have an effect on eternity. Only eternal significance lasts forever.

Review the four principles that successful people live by:

*Live your life in faith.*

*Know God has a plan for you.*

*Become a person of prayer.*

*Have an eternal focus.*

These four principles are the foundation to conquering your fear. Their power has been proven in our ancestors' success. And they continue to fuel the successful today. You will find the ultimate source of power in them. When you adopt these principles and make them a part of who you are, you will ensure your success includes peace, courage, focus, and significance. You will not only conquer your fear, you will transform your success from your good to God's best.

## Revealing The Truth About Success And Failure

Knowing the truth about success and failure is your ticket to freedom! When you adopt empowering beliefs about success and about failure, you give yourself the fuel to change your behaviors. You will begin behaving, acting, and reacting in ways that will cause you to be successful.

With your personal action plan, you will finally interrupt the bad habits you have and begin to attract and achieve all you say you want! Let the next two chapters be your personal action plan to help you conquer every fear you may have toward success or failure.

"Many of life's failures are the result of people who did not realize how close they were to success when they gave up."

—Thomas Edison

*"A failure is a man who blundered, but is not able to cash in on the experience."*

*—Elbert Hubbard*

*Chapter 7*
# Conquer Your Fear of Failure

Fear of failure can put you in a state of paralysis. You never dream big because you don't want to have to risk. You don't complete your goal, so you won't have to face the thought of possibly failing at it.

Maybe you've been hurt before in a relationship, so you fear loss, rejection or being unacceptable. Maybe you've experienced violence in your relationships and because of it you don't like confrontation.

Whatever your experience or situation, you can break through your fear of failure by knowing the truth about it. When you adopt empowering beliefs about failure, you will learn to step on each failure, using them as stepping stones guiding you to your success.

## Change Your View Of Failure And Your Fear Of It Will Change

Mark and I had just gotten married. We were in love and acting like typical newlyweds. Then, just two weeks after we said "I do," it happened—we got in our first big fight.

I can still remember the scene. I yelled something mean, marched out of the apartment, slammed the door behind me, and thought, "This must be what divorce feels like!"

Now, I know you are laughing at this. But I really felt that. You see, my parents never fought in front of us kids. Because of that I believed that couples who fight are couples who split.

Sound ridiculous? It sure is! But, this is the same principle going on in your head when you think that a failure is your sign to quit and divorce yourself from your goal.

## Truths About Failure

*Failures are the steps you take that bring you to success.*

*Failure helps you to depend on others more.*

*Failure can help bring you closer to God.*

*Failure is a small part of the big picture.*

*If you have not had a failure in the last year, you are not growing enough.*

*Growing hurts. But not growing destroys.*

*Failure is a teacher to show you what not to do.*

*Failure is a great way to help you say "I'm sorry" more.*

*Failure is a way to show you that you can't do it alone.*

*Failure is a sign that you need to stop, assess, and change.*

*Failure is a part of life.*

*Failure was never intended to kill you or to stop you.*

Add your own empowering truths about failure:

_____

_____

_____

When you get it into your head that failure is a part of your journey to success—that it is inevitable and necessary to the process—you will begin to withstand the temptation to quit when you have your first fight, hear your first no, or experience your first setback. You will not succumb to self-doubt, depression, and worry with your very first no, or your eighty-first no.

*"The difference between great-ness and mediocrity is often how an individual views a mistake."*
—*Nelson Boswell*

# Reject Rejection

Rejection to the sales person is the greatest form of failure. You feel the pang of failure with every no you get. It is the one thing that will keep you frozen like an ice sculpture, incapable of movement. Immobilized until you just melt away.

No one would want to be rejected, right? Wrong! There is one kind of person who doesn't mind rejection. In fact, this person counts on it—even looks for it and welcomes it!

That person is someone who understands the law of averages. He or she knows that it takes ten rejections to one success. Once you know the truth about the law of averages, you will never look at rejection in the same darkness. You know that rejection is a necessary part of your journey to success.

I guess you have to ask yourself, "Am I willing to hear the noes to get to the yeses? If you can't answer that in the affirmative, then get out of the sales business. The law of averages never lies, and it must be accepted and followed to ensure success.

When I was working with Mary Kay, Inc., I figured out my law of averages—the number of contacts to number of sales. It was ten to one. For every ten contacts I made, one person would agree to a selling appointment.

Then I figured out that the company's national average for sales at each appointment was about $200.

I had several copies of a twenty-dollar bill made and gave them to each person in my unit. Then I asked them, "If, on average, you make $200 at every selling appointment and it takes ten noes to get one yes, then how much money are you making on each and every no?

They replied, "Twenty bucks."

I held up the copies of the twenty-dollar bill and instructed them to tape one to their telephone. Every time they got a no, they were to hang up and say, "Thanks for the twenty bucks!"

Can you imagine the power that comes from knowing and embracing the law of averages? You won't get frustrated or stuck from a no. You will understand it's simply part of getting a yes! And if you noticed, the money is in getting the noes!

I've often wondered why men seem to accept the law of averages principle better than women do. Maybe it's because it is far more common for a parent to take their little boy outside, give them a baseball bat, and say, "Now, son, you're going to miss the ball more times than you hit the ball." That is a picture of the law of averages. You will strike out, get a no, face rejection and deal with failure more times than you will hit a homer, get a yes, make a sale, or have a success.

Be willing to bear some discomfort. Every journey toward a goal has some inherent unpleasantness. If you are in the sales industry, rejection and failure are inevitable. In fact, in just living, rejection and failure are inevitable. All people, of every race, in every career, of all ages, have to deal with failure. Embracing the law of averages and focusing on your efforts is the salesperson's secret to success.

When Auriana was five years old and learning how to tie her shoes, I told her, "Now, Auriana, it will probably take you twenty-seven times to tie your shoe before you can do it just right." This truth helped her deal with the frustration of not being able to tie that bow the first, second, or twenty-second time. What I didn't realize is how well she listened, because a few days later she came running up to me and said, "Mommy, you were wrong! It only took me eighteen times to tie my shoe just right!"

The frustration that she would have had was eliminated when she knew that she would mess up more times than she would get it right. My giving her a number, twenty-seven times (which I arbitrarily chose) freed her from a confused frustration. It gave her something concrete to focus on.

It's the same with you. If you review your past sales and come up with the average—how many contacts it takes for you to get a yes— then you can focus on those efforts, breaking them down in daily "do-ables." You eliminate the frustration of getting a no because you don't look at it as a rejection, but one step closer to a yes.

Embrace the law of averages! Know exactly what you have to do to get the results you want. How many noes do you need to accept in order to get to a yes? Write out a specific plan for yourself. Your success will be inevitable because the law of averages never lies. When you embrace the law of averages, you will stop fearing the word no and begin to respect it. Put enough noes in your life so that you just won't be afraid of rejection anymore.

Write down the number of contacts you need to make in order to get a yes.

---

Embracing the law of averages also helps you change your negative belief about the word no.

When I hear a salesperson say "I never take no for an answer!" I just cringe. Engaging in this guerrilla-style sales is one of the biggest reasons salespeople quit in the middle of their success.

When you respect the word no and allow people to say no to you, you have just helped your own mind-set. You don't have to be this bossy, forceful sales-person, twisting arms and refusing to take no for an answer.

Think of it, if after you have explained your product, given all the benefits, and done all you can to make a potential customer want to say yes, and they still say no, then, for heaven's sake, move on! Do you really want them in your life as your client or in your organization if they really don't want to be there? No! Move on to someone else who wants to be there. You miss too many people who want your product when you waste time trying to convince those who really don't.

When you create an atmosphere of respect for the word no, you will not only help yourself approach people with confidence, but you will also start to attract people to you. You will see yourself as a genuine vessel of information and opportunity for the "right" person. Others will see you as this, too, and be attracted to you. Respecting the word no can help you regain your courage.

# *Regain Your Courage*

Your lack of courage is costing you—a lot! Lack of courage is affecting your relationships, your sales, your level of success, and your ability to live an authentic life. It is your lack of courage that keeps you from the relationship you always wanted. It is lack of courage that stops you from picking up that 3,000-pound telephone and asking for the sale. It's your lack of courage that keeps you from receiving your promotion. And, it's a lack of courage that keeps you from doing something a little outrageous to get what you want.

People who lack courage have lost a most important thing: hope. And when someone loses hope, they lose the most powerful motivator that drives all success. Without hope, people fall into despair. They actually become blind to opportunity. This life of despair becomes a habit. But, just like all habits, you can reverse this negative behavior by changing your belief.

Do you believe in your dreams? Do you believe in yourself? Do you believe in a living, loving God and His limitless power? Do you believe that you have all you need to make your life work? Do you believe you have access to all power, through the One who created power? Do you believe you have unlimited courage through your natural, risk-taking ability?

No? Well, you used to! Think back to when you were a child. You had an incredible capacity for courage and hope. When you were a child, your hopes fueled your behaviors. Your amazement with life fueled your actions. Your risk-taking ability helped you believe there was nothing you couldn't do! This belief was no accident. This belief wasn't even out of the ordinary. All people are created with a natural, risk-taking ability.

Picture this: A one-year-old boy sees a set of stairs for the first time. What do you think went through his mind as he stood looking up at this exciting, new thing? (If you have ever been around kids, you know!) He probably thought to himself, "Wow! I've got to get to the top!"

He didn't stand at the bottom and think, "I'd like to get to the top, but I'd better not. I might get hurt." Or, "What would my mom say? I might get in trouble." He didn't stand at the bottom and think, "I want to get to the top . . . but, what would my friends say about me? They might laugh at me." He didn't tell himself any of these negatives. No! He just began. He focused on his goal and did not allow any negative thought to break his concentration on this wonderful new apparatus.

All of you reading this know the feelings of joy and excitement that consumed this little child as he pondered the stairwell—because this story is about YOU! You were once a child with so much amazement about things that you, too, stood at the bottom of stairs and thought, "Wow! I've got to get to the top!"

We were all born with a natural risk-taking ability. Think of two toddlers who meet each other for the first time. They don't have to know each other's names to be playmates; they just jump in and play. They don't view this as a big risk, because risking is just part of their everyday life. Fear of risking doesn't exist to a child. All people were created to risk. All people have a natural, God-given risk-taking ability.

We start off being creatures of hope, laughter, and great courage. But now, to most of you reading this book, life has had its way with you! Your circumstances, the culture, self-limiting beliefs, bad habits, and negative people have conspired to bring on a sense of sobriety. They crush your childlike thinking and adventurous spirit in ways that are too difficult to overcome and too plentiful to count.

This safe way of living, however, is not your inborn nature! You were created to risk! You were created to dream! Dreaming and risk-taking are your nature. You need to seek out risks and develop your courage. When you make dreaming, risk-taking, a sense of amazement, laughter, courage, and fun a part of your life, you will find your natural, inborn state. It's up to you to make these a part of your day. The great thing about this truth is that one courageous act leads to another, creating a courageous mentality.

Rekindle your natural risk-taking ability. Do something a little outrageous today! There's something about the willingness to occasionally go way out that reminds us of how big and abundant life can be.

Stephen Covey, author of *Seven Habits of Highly Effective People*, once said, "Out of true deep character lies the power of courage, which is the foundation of success."

One day as I was getting ready for a presentation for the Woman's Business Association, Auriana (who was four at the time) walked up to me and made a unique request. I was going to be sharing the platform with several "celebrities" on that day and my kids wanted to be a part of it all.

"Would you get a picture of you with Mary Hart?" she asked. This might seem like a strange request for a four-year-old—unless you knew that Mary Hart had recorded an album of lullabies which we listen to every night. So, Mary Hart was, at that time, right up there with other celebrities like Mickey Mouse and Barney!

"Of course I will!" I said as I kissed her good-bye.

Later that day, after Mary Hart's presentation, I went up to her and made my simple request. She looked at her publicist who looked at his watch and she replied, "I'm sorry. I don't have time for a picture." And she began to walk away.

"What?" I thought to myself, "no time for a picture?" I knew I had to think fast and do something a little outrageous to get what I wanted. The next thing I knew I stood there in the hotel lobby in front of hundreds of people and began to sing a song... not just any song, but one of the songs on Mary Hart's CD. I sang the song she wrote to her son A.J.

Mary Hart swung around with a look of surprise. Smiling, she said, "I think I have time for one picture!"

What are you willing to do that's a little outrageous, a little out of the ordinary to get what you want? Have more courage! Be willing to step out of your comfort zone and try something different. Your life just might need a crazy act to bounce you out of a rut. Your career just might need an act of outrageousness to get you off and going again. Your marriage just might need something out of the ordinary to jolt you out of a boring routine.

What are you willing to do that's a little outrageous to get your courage muscles back into shape? You can begin to create a courageous mentality with just one outrageous act.

## Cultivate Your Childlike Thinking

Research tells us that over half of a person's thoughts are filled with everyday "stuff" like returning phone calls, paying bills, making contacts, cleaning the house, getting kids to school, and what's next on their to-do lists.

We are often so swept up in your everyday routine, that we fail to see the possibilities put right in front of us. Research also tells us that over half of sales-people miss out on opportunity simply because they are not awake to it.

One of the ways to break this cycle and cultivate your risk-taking ability is to rekindle your childlike awareness! Let yourself be amazed with life again. Think of the woman who started her own business. She has an irresistible childlike outlook on her new adventure. Or the boss who has cultivated his childlike thinking in the way he leads and motivates his people. Or the parent who has a sense of fun and adventure in their parenting role.

One day, as I sat outside with my daughter, she said, "Mom, did you know there's no such thing as a baby butterfly?" Seeing my confused stare, she continued, "The caterpillar comes out of the cocoon and is an adult butterfly. It is never a baby." She's right. Children are so brilliant and awake to the unique. What about you? What will you discover, appreciate or find amazement with today? Have a sense of wonder! Scripture tells us that every star has a name. Wow! Explore the wonders of your Creator. Become intensely alive to the big and little enjoyments that life has to offer to the eye, ear, nose, tongue, and skin. When you cultivate your childlike thinking and begin to find amazement with life, you will awaken a creative side that sees opportunity and possibilities to which the average person is blind.

# Practice Extravagant Thinking

Resist saying, "Real life just isn't that way." If you have a relationship with God, you aren't in the real life. You are in the supernatural powers of God. Resist the temptation to always play it safe. Resist saying, "I'm too old for that"; or "I don't have the time for it"; or "I tried it before and it didn't work." Give yourself permission to have some adventurous fun! Sometimes you just have to splurge with your money, your imagination, and your heart. Often these grand gestures determine the course of your life. It's not just the flower that can make life interesting, but the willingness to admire and smell the flower that makes life adventurous. Extravagant thinking leads you to extravagant love, people, and things. You will begin to attract extravagance in your life.

Do you allow time for serendipity in your structured schedule? Or is your to-do list so long that there's no time left for surprises? Do you allow yourself time for fun? When was the last time you laughed? I mean really laughed—afrom the belly, grab your middle kind of laugh? I once heard it said that to maintain one's health you need to laugh out loud ten seconds every day. That's just to maintain health. What if you need to restore health? How many seconds of laughing out loud every day is needed for that?

When you laugh, your body releases a natural substance with morphine-like qualities. These natural antibodies are called endorphins, your own powerful source for staying healthy, happy, creative and alive!

Think of it, humans are the only creature with the ability to laugh. We are the only animal created to use and enjoy a sense of humor! So, use this unique gift. Put more laughter in your day! Put more adventure in your day. You are the only person who will make your life more exciting.

# The Show

The alarm clock began to ring violently. After the maddening noise could no longer be ignored, I reluctantly pulled myself out of bed to turn it off. It was only 4:30 am—too early to get up on a holiday. But, I had promised my three children we would spend this morning on the beach watching the sun come up.

They, of course, jumped right out of bed excited to "see the show" as they called it. As I finished my shower my slumber began to dissipate, and before I knew it we were all sitting on a blanket, eyes glued to the horizon in anticipation of the great show. It was 6:05 a.m.

Just fifteen minutes later, our eyes, still fixed on the horizon, experienced the most beautiful sight we have ever seen.

"Look mom! The sun makes the clouds purple—your favorite color!" Beau yelled.

"This is better than fireworks!" Auriana screamed. "Wow! Does this happen every morning Mom?" Connor asked.

Yes! It happens every morning. When was the last time you "saw the show?" We are exposed to so much man-made beauty. But, too often, we forget to include the most awesome adventure of all—the unique, authentic, God-given treasure of nature!

Next time you have a day off, don't forget to see the show. It just might change the way you look at life that day.

# Dream Extravagantly

It takes courage to dream big. This courage will grow when you pursue your curiosity. When you follow where your curiosity leads you, you rediscover a creative side to you that has been long forgotten.

When was the last time you said, "I've got a crazy idea!" Don't be too proud to follow your curiosity. In Bill Gates' biography, he is quoted as saying, "We tell our people that if they don't get at least three people who laugh at their idea, they're probably not being creative enough." Have the courage to pursue your curiosity and dream big!

The only difference between a dream and reality is ACTION. Unfulfilled dreams are just dreams that were never followed through with action. The danger in these unfulfilled dreams is that they begin to affect your success in other areas your life.

What dream did you put off? Learning how to play the piano? Visiting a far off country? Taking dance lessons? Being a baseball star? What action could you take right toward fulfilling these dreams?

What small step toward your dream could you take right now? I can't tell you enough how strongly this small step of action could affect your success equation and create your success mind-set. Decide which small step of action you will take today to turn your dream into reality.

Call a piano teacher. Sign up for the city's baseball league (even if it's the over forty league!) Take a night class. Get a foreign language tutor. Call a travel agent. Research the internet. This small, extra effort just might be the one thing that will catapult you into an outrageous, courageous, risk-taker!

## Take A Courageous Account

Another great way to cultivate your risk-taking ability is to think back on what you have already done. What have you done when you called on your courage that surprised even you! The human condition is about surviving under unmentionable odds! We all have our stories about courageous acts.

When I ask my audiences what was the most outlandish, courageous thing they've ever done, the stories that get shouted out are incredible! One lady said, "I bought a sailboat and I don't even know how to sail. I just love the water and want to be out and around it as much as I can. So, I bought the boat and now have to learn how to be a sailor."

Another lady jumped up and shouted, "I met a man in a bar, fell in love, and married him!" This conservative woman ignored what "they" said, took a chance and it worked.

One man yelled, "I took a sabbatical and back-packed around Europe for a year!"

A very shy young woman stood and said, "I had a dinner party for my three friends, and for the first time in eight years I entertained people in my home."

What have you done that was courageous? Risk-taking is like beauty. It's all in the eyes of the beholder. What may be a big risk to one is easy to another. Don't compare your risk level with others. Compare it with what you've done in the past.

List the seven most courageous things you've ever done:

_____     _____

_____     _____

_____     _____

_____

# *Dreams Mixed With A Vision = Reality*

Years ago, when I was in a direct sales company, I set a goal at the company's convention to achieve Court of Sales by the next year's convention. The first thing I did to help me achieve this seemingly impossible goal was to create my vision of success.

I went backstage at the end of that year's convention—when the auditorium was empty—and walked onto that stage looking out at the 10,000 empty seats. I pictured myself in a royal blue and silver gown walking down the fifteen steps (I counted them!) to a cheering auditorium filled with my friends, colleagues, and family. I played that powerful picture in my mind over and over again and created an emotional attachment to that goal. On those days when I just didn't feel like picking up that 3,000-pound telephone to make another sales call, I would again visualize those fifteen steps, play that scene I had created in my mind, and find the enthusiasm to focus and continue.

A year later, I did walk on that stage living out the vision that I had acted out in my mind throughout the past twelve months! The cheering friends, the money made, and the sense of pride could not have occurred without that sixty-second vision I had created and played back so many times over that year.

Truly spiritual people have the freedom to dream. They know that nothing they dream is too difficult for them because they believe God will provide all they need to complete it. They think differently, believe differently, dream differently, and act differently. And because of their expanded mindset, they receive God's abundance.

God wants His people to be set a part from the world. While many of life's situations call for seriousness, your circumstances do not have to rob you of your joy or of your expanded mindset. Even in difficult situations you can experience joy and continue to dream big through an abundant God, who loves you and wants to bless you.

I know this type of belief is not popular in our world today. So much of our joy is based on what we have, not on who has us. So much of our peace is based on what we can accomplished, not on whose working through us. You can draw your courage from this one fact: You belong to God and He is desperately in love with you. God's very nature is abundance. And He wants to share His abundance with people who BELIEVE in Him and who ASK of Him.

I once heard a fable about a man who found an enormous building in heaven. Inside the building, he found rows and rows of neatly stacked boxes, each tied with a satin bow. When the man found the box with his name on it, he quickly tore it open. Inside his box, he found all the blessings that God wanted to give to him while he was one earth... but had never asked.

Have you ever asked God for His blessings? Have you ever asked God to expand your business? When was the last time God worked through you in such a way that you knew, beyond doubt, God had done it?

When you ask of Him, His power will manifest. The bigger the request, the bigger the need for Him and His power. Have the courage to dream big and ask for God's rich blessing over your dream. It is your opportunity to make an invisible God visible.

God's bounty is not reserved just for apostles, prophets, or Biblical scholars. His opulent blessings are limited only by you and your willingness to ask.

Through a simple, believing prayer, you can change your future. I couldn't recommend more highly living than in this supernatural dimension!

*"Failure isn't so bad if it doesn't attack the heart. Success is all right if it doesn't go to the head."*

—Grantland Rice

*"I'd rather be a failure at something I enjoy than be a success at something I hate."*

*—George Burns*

# Chapter 8
# Conquer Your Fear of Success

Most people secretly link a tremendous amount of hidden pain to being successful. Their beliefs about success are terrifying! The real danger is they don't even realize they have a fear of success. After all, who would think that success would be feared? We were all raised to desire success. Or were we? For many, it's not the fear of failure that keeps them from their full potential. It is their fear of *really making it*!

Nelson Mandela, in an excerpt of his 1994 inaugural address said the following:

*Our deepest fear is not that we are inadequate.*
*Our deepest fear is that we are powerful beyond measure.*
*It is our light, not our darkness that most frightens us.*
*We ask ourselves, who am I to be brilliant, gorgeous, talented and fabulous?*

*Actually, who are you not to be?*
*You are a child of God.*

*Your playing small does not serve the world.*
*There's nothing enlightening about shrinking so that other people won't feel insecure around you.*

*We are born to manifest the glory of God that is within us. It's not just in some of us; it's in everyone.*

*And as we let our own light shine, we unconsciously give other people permission to do the same.*

*As we are liberated from our own fear, our presence automatically liberates others.*

These words from Nelson Mandela hit me hard. For me, it wasn't the fear of failure that kept me from risking and pursuing my dreams. It was the fear of letting the brightness within me shine!

I resigned my position as a school teacher to be a full-time mom and housewife nearly thirteen years ago. When my third child started school, I began to work on a home-based business. The business quickly grew in size, and I had to hire an assistant to help me manage the rapid growth.

My life looked ideal—on the outside. But inside, I was in turmoil. I didn't feel like I was successful at all. I didn't "fit" into my new life of business success.

"How can I be a good parent with this success?" was one of my secret thoughts. "I don't deserve all this." was another. At the same time I said things like, "How can I get everything done?" "There are so many people depending on me now." I felt like the more I achieved, the greater the pressure to maintain my success. I would often remind myself, "Who am I to think I can run such a successful business? I've been 'just a mom' for so long."

I found little peace or fulfillment in my success. The demons from my negative beliefs about success overshadowed the joy of accomplishment.

Even though I was successful in the world's eyes, I knew there was something missing. My success story could have been so much better.

Like me, you may fear being top salesperson and having to maintain that success. You may fear a commitment to marriage, and all the responsibility that it involves. You may fear really succeeding in your business and dealing with being at the top with no where to go but down (or so you believe). You may fear that you don't deserve success and one day you will be "found out".

If you feel like you just don't measure up and you believe you are not doing enough, working enough, spending enough time with the kids or your spouse, praying enough, making enough, or are enough to be successful, then a large amount of the time, you don't like yourself. You are in a private war that affects everything you do.

I was enslaved in the same war with my own self-limiting beliefs and my fear of success. It wasn't until that day in Bermuda when I faced my fear of success that I could be free. It wasn't my husband, my family, the way I was raised, the company, the culture, or the economy, that was keeping me from enjoying my success. It was me. It was my fear, self-limiting beliefs, and lack of faith. I was the only person who could change these three success assassins.

## Make The Commitment

The first thing I did to conquer my fear of success was I began to cultivate my faith. I made a commitment to spend time with God every day. I began to discern what I was taught about God in my childhood with what I chose to believe in my adulthood. I studied my religion. And what I discovered was *my faith is my power*.

The day I finally came to the understanding that my career, my family, this book project, and my life is not about me, was the day I found freedom! The moment I gave up control and gave it to the One who created me, was the moment I was free to dream, risk, and fulfill my destiny. When I put my faith in God's plan for me, there is no failure.

It was when I cultivated my faith that I could knock out the noise of my self-limiting beliefs and hear the clear direction from the One who has my success story written out. From this strong faith, I had the courage to begin the next steps in my breakthrough.

# Three Steps To Your Breakthrough

My breakthrough consisted of three steps. First, I had to expose my true fear and admit that what I was really afraid of was success. Secondly, I began to reveal the negative beliefs and the lies I had connected with success. Thirdly, I replaced the negative beliefs with empowering ones and adopted a powerful belief system. Following these three steps, coupled with your growing faith, is how you too, will conquer your fear and achieve what you really want.

*1. Expose your true fear*

*2. Reveal the negative beliefs*

*3. Adopt an empowering belief system*

## Step 1: Expose the true fear

"Fear of pain may be worse than pain itself" was the conclusion scientist, Dr. Alexander Ploghaus came to in a study done at Britain's Oxford University. His report, published in the New York Times in 1999, suggests that the fear of being afraid is far worse than any of the actual events of fear. In other words, the fear of rejection is far worse than the actual rejection. The fear of commitment is far worse than actually committing to someone or something. The fear of failure is far worse than actually failing at something. The fear of risk is far worse than actually taking a risk. The fear of success is far worse than actually succeeding. Franklin D. Roosevelt's quote from his inaugural address has never rang more true, "The only thing we have to fear is fear itself."

That tiny eight-word quote spoke volumes to me! When I realized the truth about fear and the negative beliefs I had about fear, I knew I was on my way.

## Step 2: Reveal the negative beliefs

The Millionaire Next Door, written by Thomas Stanley, Ph.D., and William Dunko, Ph.D., helped me begin the process of revealing and replacing my negative beliefs about success. This book opened my eyes to a new definition of the American millionaire.

According to their research, 92 percent of America's millionaires are married; and of those married, 95 percent have children and are a part of traditional families. One in four American millionaires have been with the same spouse for thirty-eight or more years! They drive cars that are a year old or older. They are hard-working, average people.

*The Millionaire Next Door* shook up my negative beliefs about success and successful people. The research shows American millionaires are people who have strong core values—very similar to our ancestors and forefathers. They value their marriage and their family and work hard at improving them. They welcome commitment and responsibility. They have the courage to bear discomfort and failure. Their lives and goals reach out beyond themselves. The profile of the American millionaire is one who knows who they are, knows their unique calling, and allows their life values to motivate every decision they make. The millionaires in America are everyday people—just like you and me.

I began to reprogram my beliefs about success. I posted the following truths about success all over my home and office and fed my mind and heart the following empowering beliefs about success.

## Truths About Success

*Success means living the life you love.*

*Success is knowing who you are in God's plan.*

*Success isn't always measured by financial gain.*

*Becoming financially secure is really about your faith in God and depending*

*upon Him to supply your needs.*

*Becoming wealthy may be a part of your success.*

*Money gives you choices.*

*Successful people have balance in their life.*

*98 percent of the millionaires in the United States have been successfully*

*married for over twenty years.*

*Successful people know how to play as well as work.*

*Success means to dream as well as act, to believe as well as plan.*

*Money is not your God.*

*The LOVE of money is the root of all evil.*

*You can have control of your time when you are successful.*

*It is possible to enjoy life and still become wealthy.*

*Success is obeying the unique plan God has for you.*

*It is possible to be a great parent and become successful.*

*If you are in a relationship with the living, loving God, you are already successful.*

I read this list of empowering beliefs about success every day and began to replace my negative beliefs. These truths began to change the way I believed about success which helped me change the way I behaved. My beliefs began to affect my behaviors.

Researching the truths about success and spending time with God helped me gain the courage to take the next step.

## 3. Adopt an empowering belief system

Hebrews 12: 1-2 says, *Let us lay aside every weight . . . and let us run with endurance the race that is set before us.*

I had laid aside every weight and negative belief about success. Now I needed to run with endurance the race that was set before me. Before I could start running, and live out my empowering beliefs, I needed to know where I was going (what was set before me).

I needed to know what my life mission was. I wanted to know I was on the right path in the right race and spending my time on the right things before I gave it my all.

It's amazing how easily people surrender their God-given hours and days in the pursuit of activities they really don't care about and have nothing to do with their life mission. Schedules and routines were made to serve you, not to rule you. There are no slaves in America.

If you do not have a clear mission and a bigger plan in mind, your activities are chosen for you. When you have a clear mission for your life, however, you will not be controlled by schedules, people, or temptations. Knowing your life mission gives you the clarity and the focus that will grow your courage. Clarity gives you focus. Focus gives you incredible courage and great confidence.

One of the best ways to know your life mission is to write down three of the most important things you want to teach your children before they leave home. If you had the opportunity to leave your kids with three core truths about life what would they be?

_____

_____

_____

Now, write six words that you would like said about you in your obituary.

_____    _____

_____    _____

_____    _____

Lastly, write a message that you would leave behind if you knew your last day was today. What would you want to tell the world with this last note?

_____

_____

_____

Look back to the list you made earlier in the book of your talents and core values. You have already been given the talent and life circumstances needed to fulfill your life mission. This "message" reflects your heart's desire and includes your talents and personal circumstances.

Hebrews 12: 1-2 says, *Let us lay aside every weight . . . and let us run with endurance the race that is set before us.*

I followed this scripture by breaking through the negative beliefs and laying aside every weight. God's purpose for me and my life mission became crystal clear through prayer and introspection. Now, I could complete the final step and run with endurance.

## Attitude Is Still Everything

Your attitude and how you choose to see yourself, your life, and others is still the deciding factor in running with endurance. When you cultivate your faith and grow your relationship with the living, loving God, your attitude will improve. You will begin to see things differently. The color within you can color the world around you. When you connect with God, He will put the beautiful color of truth and knowledge in you. And beautiful things will inevitably come out.

Psalms 139: 17 says, *How precious are your thoughts about me, O God! I can't even count them; they out number the grains of sand!*

God's thoughts about you are precious and numerous. When you choose to take hold of this truth, you will begin to live a rich life. When you choose to live a rich life, you feel rich in every way. You act expansively and generously with your time, love, and money and these things respond to you in the same way. In order to truly experience a rich life, you have to adopt the truth that God is desperately in love with you. When you take hold of this truth you will live differently. You will raise your standards for yourself and your life. You will value life and surround yourself with only the things that you value. You can not feel poor and undeserving and expect to live a rich life. When you value who you are and what you do, the world will value you.

## *Raise Your Standards*

I believe people who have a rich life have it not because they have every material pleasure you could think of. They have a rich life because they are not afraid to really live and to really love! They want to give their family, their career, their hobbies, and their life all they've got. They have high standards for their life in every area. They have a high standard for a healthy, happy family. So they do what it takes to commit the time and energy to achieve that. They have a high standard for their finances. So they learn about investing and follow through with their education. They have a high standard for their spiritual life. So they spend time with God daily and study His Word.

Balance comes from having a high standard for your self and your lifestyle. You deserve the very best life you can possibly offer. God calls us to heaven on earth. I'm not talking about the "name it and claim it" philosophy, which is what many churches teach their congregations. What I am talking about is to expect the best, create high standards for your life, then do all you can to assist God in creating it.

*"You may have to fight a battle more than once to win it."*
—Margaret Thatcher

*"Champions keep playing until they get it right."*
—Billy Jean King

# Have Endurance In The Process

Endurance means to continue in the race no matter how difficult. The problem comes when we want success NOW! We rush the process. Have more confidence in the process. It takes time to improve. It takes time to change habits. It takes time to alter beliefs. It takes time to create success. The only step that takes an instant is making the decision. It is after taking that step you must commit to the process.

Don't rush the process. Endurance is an important step in the journey. When you start to get frustrated with the process, call on your faith and your discipline to get you through this time of burnout.

# The Success Cycle

I remember when my seven-year-old son, Beau, started telling me he didn't want to do his homework anymore. Daily he would lament, "I don't feel like doing this!" It was such a change from the excited little first-grader who couldn't wait to receive and complete his new assignments! To get him to succeed in his schoolwork, I decided to use one of the success philosophies I teach in my sales training: Success is a cycle of enthusiasm and discipline.

All successes are fueled by enthusiasm. It's contagious! Enthusiasm helps you accomplish tasks with ease. But when you don't feel so enthused, the second success cycle, discipline, must kick in. I shared with Beau the times I don't feel like doing my phone work or mailing out promotional packs or doing the laundry... but I just begin anyway. The amazing thing is that discipline breeds results and results breed enthusiasm. It is a continuous cycle... "The Success Cycle."

What do you do when you've lost your enthusiasm, when you don't feel like doing the work needed to grow, or completing the necessary tasks to meet success? I challenge you to call on your discipline to get through that stage. Decide how many efforts you will accomplish that day. Maybe it's ten phone calls or fifteen minutes of effort. When you can discipline yourself to make some efforts—even small efforts towards your goal—your enthusiasm begins to rekindle. The cycle continues.

The cycle of success can be compared to the recycling symbol, with its three arrows moving clockwise. In the success cycle, the arrows represent discipline, results, and enthusiasm. All three are needed in the equation of success.

When I acknowledged Beau's negative feelings and replied, "Sometimes you have to do things you don't want to do," he sat down to complete half of his assignment fired by discipline. After half was done, he noticed the results and completed the rest of the assignment with enthusiasm.

The reality in this success cycle is that when you call on discipline to help you complete a task, your enthusiasm floods back. You'll be on fire once again... until the next time!

What small steps are you willing to take even when burnout is resting on your shoulders? Rely on your discipline to take you through the fire. Then, you, like Beau, are just a few short steps from reveling in your enthusiasm.

Endurance is a learned behavior. It doesn't come naturally. It has to be practiced. When you do experience burnout along the way, remember this: Just like a candle, you can't be burned out without having once been on fire. Let your discipline be the catalyst that gets you back to being on fire again. Allow your time of frustration to be an opportunity for reevaluation, introspection, or a time to look to God for your strength. Balance your enthusiasm with discipline and you will run with endurance.

Have more faith. You will conquer your fears when you cultivate your faith. Lay aside every weight, and break through the negative, self-limiting beliefs you have about success or failure. Adopt an empowering belief system, and know the truth about God's abundant love for you and His great plan for your life.

The truth will set you free to run with endurance, power, and clarity, the race that is set before you.

# *Epilogue*

Until our paths cross again, I want to leave you with this last thought ...

When you do meet your goals and experience your success, remember it's not the prize that you will truly cherish. No, it's not the prize. It's the pride! It's the pride of who you became through the process and what you learned along the way. It's the pride in knowing that you had the opportunity to make an invisible God visible. God's ultimate power was shown in your life when you chose to find your faith, befriend your fear, dream big dreams and adopt an empowering belief system, so you could become the person you were intended to be. Then you can be proud of the legacy that you left behind!

God's richest blessings,
Lisa Jimenez

P.S. Thank you for taking this journey with me. I have shared a lot of my personal struggles and successes with you. I want to invite you to do the same. Get in contact with me and share your story. I would love to hear how this book has made a difference in your life. My email address is Lisa@conquer-fear.com. If you would like me to speak at your next convention or to view my on-line superstore go to www.conquer-fear.com.

# The Seven Truths

### Truth #1
**Fear is the dominant problem in your life today.**

### Truth #2
**Fear is a gift that was instilled in you as a means of protection and a way to bring you closer to God.**

### Truth #3
**When you run from or deny your fear, you leave the gift unopened.**

### Truth #4
**When your fear of success or fear of failure is exposed, you break through their control over you.**

### Truth #5
**Your belief system is the driving force behind your behaviors and your results.**

### Truth #6
**Your everyday habits are broadcasting your belief system, your fear, and your unmet needs loud and clear.**

### Truth # 7
**Change your beliefs and you change your behaviors.**
**Change your behaviors and you change your results.**
**Change your results and you change your life.**

# About the Author

Lisa Jimenez has helped thousands of top salespeople shatter their self-limiting beliefs and finally get the breakthrough success they want. When it comes to personal productivity and creating unstoppable momentum, there is no one better for your salespeople than Lisa.

Her fast-paced, powerful programs come directly from her real-life experience of building a successful direct sales business of her own. Because of this experience, your people will identify with Lisa's personal stories and get the message.

They will laugh out loud when Lisa reveals the hidden messages that are in the most common fears of all salespeople. They will be empowered, through her insight and humor, to identify these fears in their own behavior and discard them forever.

Lisa penetrates the hearts of your audience when she reveals her own experience breaking through self-limiting beliefs and turned them into the driving force behind her success. Just nine months later, she used these new beliefs to sign a six-figure consulting contract.

From her doctoral work in leadership at Florida Atlantic University, to her matchless experience building a business herself, to her home life as a wife and mother of three children, Lisa gives your people a fun, powerful message of life and work success. They will regain their drive, childlike courage, risk-taking ability, and get "on fire" for what they have to offer in creating personal and career success.

Lisa is the author of four tape albums and two books covering personal and professional development.

If you are ready to shatter self-limiting beliefs and conquer your fear forever... If you are ready to be encouraged and challenged to reach new levels of success ... then you need to bring in Lisa Jimenez for your next rally or convention. Call today at 1-800-489-7391 or (954) 755-3670 to book Lisa, or go to www.conquer-fear.com.

# For Meeting Planners

Dear Meeting Planner,

Welcome! Thank you for considering one of my breakthrough programs for your next event. I would love to work with you and offer your clients a motivational, thought-provoking, fun program that is rich with content and humor. I work with sales people who want to become more productive by breaking through their procrastination, fear, and self-limiting beliefs to sell much more.

Here's what I want you to know more than anything else...

I know firsthand the freedom that comes from exposing and eliminating the fear of success and fear of failure. And I will do whatever it takes to make sure your people get and live this message. When I'm done with them, they will know that it is only when they break through their fears that they can be freed-up to accept success, attract opportunity, and live their full potential.

My message and personal stories have empowered thousands of people to figure out why they do what they do, and then have the courage to change those bad habits and self-sabotaging behaviors to finally achieve all they say they want and live the life they love!

The most effective way to ensure continued learning and change is to provide your people with a source for that ongoing learning. That is why I offer an ultimate success package which includes an autographed copy of my book, Conquer Fear! Ending Procrastination to Achieve What You Really Want! with every speaking engagement. That means when you bring me in for your next event, your people will not only walk out pumped up, focused and ready to achieve their goals, they will also be equipped for long-term success with my powerful message in their own copy of my book Conquer Fear!

Your people will learn how to adopt a powerful belief system that will energize them like a multi-vitamin and help them create their personal career path to accomplish all they say they want and live the life they love!

146

I provide you with first-class, professional programs and materials—that I'm happy to customize for you and I'm easy to work with. Give me a call personally and I'll be happy to discuss dates and help you make your next event a spectacular success!

Warmly,
Lisa Jimenez, M.Ed.

P.S. When you want your people to become more productive and sell more, call Lisa to open your next conference with a customized, personal, humor-based keynote. Call today at (800) 489-7391 or (954) 755-3670 or check out our website at www.conquer-fear.com.

# Programs Offered by Lisa Jimenez:

- *Break Through Your Comfort Zone to the Success Zone*
- *Conquer Fear! Rejecting Rejection to Achieve What You Really Want*
- *Radical Recruiting! How to Find, Attract and Sponsor the Winners!*
- *How to Lead and Empower Others*

## Break Through Your Comfort Zone to the Success Zone

One of the greatest secrets to success is getting out of your comfort zone and doing the things most people are not willing to do. This can be terrifying to some people. Lisa shows your people how to overcome this fear and tap into their natural talents and bring out the best in themselves and others.

In this fun, information-packed program, your sales force will learn the personal development strategies and sales skills they need to master the business and achieve their goals. They will learn how to:

- *Cultivate their innate abilities;*
- *Believe in their dream;*
- *Have the courage to take risks;*
- *Attract opportunity;*
- *Create a laser focus;*
- *Build healthier relationships; and,*
- *Explode out of their self-imposed limitations to accept success!*

Lisa uses humor, case studies and her personal experience to give your people courage. They will develop the courage that empowers them to pick up that 3,000-pound telephone, approach more prospects and close more sales!

Book this program for your next sales meeting or convention and let Lisa teach your sales force the steps to strengthen their courage—so they can break through their comfort zone to the success zone!

## Conquer Fear!
## Rejecting Rejection to Achieve What You Really Want

The biggest barrier that all sales distributors have to overcome is fear. Fear of rejection. Fear of making decisions. Fear of change. Fear of failure. And of course the big one: Fear of success! It is this fear (and all of its cousins like worry, anxiety, and self-doubt) that paralyzes your people and keeps them from succeeding.

This program will give your sales force a practical action plan to empower them to befriend their fear, reject rejection, and be free to get on with creating and achieving what they want! Lisa will guide them in an understanding of why they do what they do.

They will laugh (and be shocked) when they discover the hidden messages that their behavior is screaming out. Through personal stories and humor, Lisa reveals the most common ways that people's belief systems can actually repel success! Lisa will show your people why positive thinking by itself just isn't enough. They will learn the steps to improve their results by developing a powerful belief system.

This program will help your people:

- *Identify and overcome self-limiting beliefs;*
- *Stop procrastination and self-sabotage;*
- *Reject rejection with the L.O.A. (law of averages);*
- *Break through negative programming;*
- *Raise their self-esteem and confidence level;*
- *Create momentum to stay motivated; and,*
- *Increase their bottom line by closing more sales.*

The power in this program comes from blending the two disciplines of psychology and spirituality. By blending the head and heart aspects of motivation, you will master the strongest combination of handling rejection and conquering your fear . . . forever!

## Radical Recruiting!  How to Find, Attract, and Sponsor the Winners!

Radical Recruiting will help you build your organization fast. You will learn an easy to duplicate 5-step recruiting process that will help you:

- *Discover and eliminate your hidden fears about prospecting;*
- *Find out where to find the best prospects;*
- *Learn how to make powerful presentations to build your image – and your confidence;*
- *Practice the best strategy for successful follow-up;*
- *Discover the secrets to overcome the toughest objections;*
- *Learn the most effective close to help your prospect say yes; and*
- *Create momentum to make building your business more fun.*

If you're serious about enrolling more leaders, making more money, and having more fun prospecting, then Radical Recruiting can show you the way. In this program, Lisa Jimenez M.Ed., digs deep to the root of prospecting to show you how to take your business to the next level. Lisa will empower you with the personal growth tools and dynamite prospecting skills you need to boost your business now! She uses her real-world experience of building a big business herself, to show you how to attract and retain the winners. Lisa's 5-step recruiting process is motivating to follow and gets results.

These are the recruiting secrets you've been searching for!

## How to Lead and Empower Others

Most people in leadership positions don't know the difference between managing their people and truly leading them. The leaders who get outrageous results from their people, do so because they have total belief in their company, product, and people. They also know how to communicate these beliefs and convictions in the most powerful way! They paint the vision so clearly and vividly that every person they lead sees that vision too, and feels they have a unique part in accomplishing it.

In this perceptive program on leadership skills, Lisa shows your people how to:

- *Use imagination and reality to achieve any goal;*
- *Turn goals into a compelling vision and communicate that vision with power;*
- *Create an emotional connection to their vision;*
- *Develop and empower others;*
- *Ignite a sense of synergy and team spirit; and,*
- *Instill autonomy in their team members.*

Lisa will teach your people how to craft a vision big enough to encompass the visions of the people they lead, communicate their vision in the most powerful way, and break down the vision into steps to take on a daily basis to bring it to reality. When you need your people to step up and lead by example, this is the program to book.

# Learning Resources by Lisa Jimenez:

- *Rich Life Kit*
- *RX Success Newsletter*
- *Craft Your Vision*
- *Journey to Self-Discovery*
- *Irresistible Leadership*
- *Creating Success*
- *Break Through Your Comfort Zone to the Success Zone*
- *Conquer Fear!*
- *Conquer Fear! Audio Album*
- *Radical Recruiting! Audio Album*
- *27 Tips to Radical Recruiting! E-Coaching Programs*

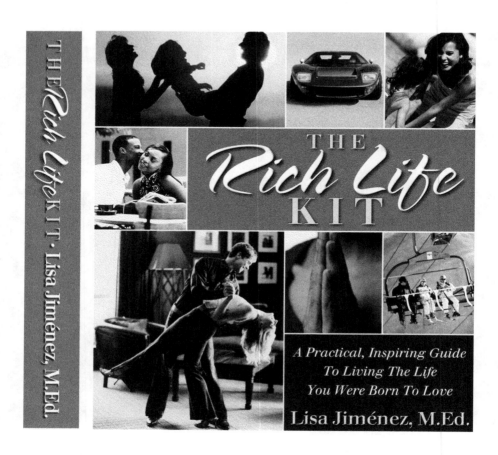

**31 – Audio CD's and Study Guide**
**Advanced 27 Day Program to Shift Your Beliefs About**
**Money, Success, and Living a Life You Love!**

## Rich Life Kit

How many times have you set a goal for yourself that you are excited about, and then, within a very short time you get side-tracked and stop doing the things you know you need to do to accomplish your goals?

Are you lazy? Do you lack discipline?

No! I don't think it is either of these. I believe it is your **beliefs** about letting yourself really live—really love—really succeed—that hold you back! Many people think they're just not meant to live an outrageous life. And that belief keeps them in bondage of mediocrity!

You were never intended to live this way . . .

Through all of the personal coaching I do, I've noticed a common thread with most of my clients: The reason behind unrealized potential is most people have a tremendous hidden fear of money and they don't feel worthy of success. So they sabotage the success they say they want!

Don't settle for a life of just getting by. Let me be your personal coach for the next 30 days and help you reveal your dreams and live beyond what you ever thought was possible.

In this 31-CD Program of The Rich Life Kit you'll learn how to:
- Cultivate the risk-taker in you:
- Be set free to dream bigger;
- Silence those annoying voices that keep you from living your rich life;
- Know what you want and find the courage to ask for it;
- Change your beliefs about wealth;
- Know the difference between confidence and self-esteem;
- Destroy doubt and cultivate your faith;
- Break through old habits that hold you back;
- Live outside yourself and your human limitations;
- Attract opportunity to you; and,
- Create an extraordinary adventure and live a life you love!

If you are ready to think differently, dream differently, and tap into your innate wisdom to build a richer life, then invest in **The Rich Life Kit** today. Take the first step to releasing the bold, adventurous, risk-taker in you!

Rich Life Kit (31 CD Program with work-a-long Study Guide) $497

# Rich Life Mastermind Retreats

Maui, Hawaii

Paris, France

**Rich Life Mastermind Retreats**
**Coaching Program for Entrepreneurs**

# Coaching Program for Entrepreneurs

What would your business look like if you spent 5 days masterminding with other entrepreneurs in the most exotic locations in the world?

We can think of no better measure of success of the Rich Life Retreat than the feedback we receive from our participants. "Best business-building experience of my life!" writes Tonya Grimes from Heritage Dolls. "My Internet sales went through the roof after I returned from the Paris Rich Life Retreat."

The Rich Life Mastermind Retreat is a unique and unforgettable experience for entrepreneurs who want to create their business or take it to the next level. First of all, they are first class, royal treatment. This is the type of rich ambience and inspiring energy that will set the stage for outrageous dream building. You will be picked up in limousines, dining in the finest restaurants on the most delectable foods, and treated like pure royal.

This royal treatment is mandatory to set the stage for the type of work we'll be doing . . .

In the Rich Life Retreat you will be tapping into the power of intuition, intention, and inspiration. Using both the head and the heart, you will discover what you really want AND a plan of action to accomplish it.

The Rich Life Retreat is highly interactive. You will be creating and planning your business venture. We will utilize the power of the mastermind and draw on the synergy of like-minded people coming together for a single purpose — to manifest our Big Dream and Rich Life!

The Rich Life Retreat promises to be the most powerful event you've ever participated in. Participate in the Rich Life Retreat and learn how to embrace and *manifest* ALL you were meant to BE and do.

For more information, call (800) 489-7391 or (954) 755-3670.

**12-audiotape album**

## Once you know your purpose...Craft Your Vision

Living the lifestyle of your dreams begins with crafting the vision of where you want to go. For without a clear, compelling vision — you simply cannot achieve what you're truly capable of. And, there simply is no better resource to help you create an empowering vision for yourself than this amazing resource. As soon as this 12-audiotape album was released, it was hailed as one of the greatest self-development tools since The Seven Habits of Highly Effective People.

You'll learn how to craft your personal vision; how to design a vision big enough to encompass the visions of your people; and steps to take on a daily basis to bring your vision to reality.

You'll hear twelve complete programs on vision—recorded live—from twelve of the foremost experts on sales, recruiting and marketing. It would cost you tens of thousands of dollars to assemble this faculty—you'll hear from all twelve of them, for less than a hundred bucks.

This breakthrough album includes talks by:

- *Richard Brooke*
- *Lisa Jimenez, M.Ed.*
- *Michael S. Clouse*
- *John Kalench*
- *Rita Davenport*
- *John David Mann*
- *John Milton Fogg*
- *Jan Ruhe*
- *Matthew Freese*
- *Tom Schreiter*
- *Randy Gage*
- *Tom Welch*

The insights on vision you'll get from this album are mind-blowing. Quite simply, this is the most powerful resource on how to craft your vision ever recorded. Make sure you get it.

**12-audiotape album**                          **Order #A2, $97**

**70-minute video and 8-page workbook**

## Take your Journey to Self-Discovery

Lisa Jimenez tells us, "Your Purpose is found in your uniqueness." This powerful videotape takes you through the process of self-discovery—knowing who you are and where you want to go. Recorded live, this intriguing program will help you discover that person who is uniquely you—and see that person unfold into your highest good.

You'll learn how to:

- *Discover your passion;*
- *Overcome procrastination;*
- *Eliminate self-destructive behavior;*
- *Start thinking on "the positive channel"; and,*
- *Develop a support system that empowers you.*

You'll experience the entire program live, just as the actual workshop attendees did. Get it now!

*"Your resources are so professional. Your message in 'Take Your Journey to Self-Discovery' was right on target and very much needed in our office staff. I have seen improvement in our staff relations and enthusiasm. I personally appreciated your philosophy that self-acceptance and authenticity always precede a business success."*
—Cheryl Roll, CHME, CHSP, Sales Manager, Great Locations Hospitality

*"You really captivated me in your video, 'Take Your Journey to Self-Discovery.' In fact, I learned a great deal about myself, as well as my coworkers. I feel more confident in my ability to relate and connect with others!"*
—Dora Shapiro, Prudential Florida

**70-minute video and 8-page workbook**          **Order #V1, $37**

**6-audiotape album and 32-page workbook**

## Creating Success

If you want to reach higher levels of success in your life — this is the resource you need. You will learn how to overcome life's challenges, build healthier relationships and create a laser focus to achieve what you want. Lisa's most powerful resource to date, this album will show you the way to success. Learn how to:

- *Identify negative belief barriers and destroy them.*
- *Eliminate bad habits by changing the beliefs that cause them.*
- *Cultivate faith. Generate the power to move mountains.*
- *Create laser focus. Ignore distractions and accomplish what you want.*
- *Change your view of failure. Learn to use failure as a stepping to success.*
- *Develop your sense of humor. Laugh your way to health and happiness.*
- *Have more courage. It's what you can learn from a lobster.*
- *Build relationships. Discover the secrets of all human relationships.*
- *Much, much more.*

*"Your six-tape, 'Creating Success' album was chocked-full of content. We've seen a powerful improvement in our mind set that has meant more sales in our department."*

—Scott Vogel, Sales & Marketing, Westin Hotels

*"Excellent piece, Lisa...I especially liked your description of the Success Cycle. It empowered me to be more persistent. I now know how to identify any belief barriers and destroy them."*

—Bill Bankowski, President, Innovative Services, Inc.

**6-audiotape album and 32-page workbook       Order #A3,$77**

**60-minute video and 8-page workbook**

## Breakthrough Your Comfort Zone To The Success Zone!
## Special Video Presentation

The secret to success is getting out of your Comfort Zone — and challenging yourself to do more. Yet, instinctively, we each fight this. We naturally want to stay in the security and safety of the familiar yet, you know to truly achieve great things, you must cross the fringe of fear and take action. This powerful video will empower you to do that. You'll learn how to:

- *Eliminate bad habits by shattering the self-limiting beliefs which cause them;*

- *Create a laser focus to ignore distractions and accomplish the things you want;*

- *Laugh your way to health and happiness;*

- *Build healthier relationships; and,*

- *Explode out of your current limitations and rocket to higher levels of achievements in both your personal and professional life!*

*"The how-to information in your video helped our division have our highest production ever! It's so true that we had some negative belief barriers that needed to be broken through."*
—Donna Sandberg, Executive Senior Sales Director, Mary Kay Cosmetics

*"Thank you for your great information in 'Moving From Your Comfort Zone to the Success Zone.' The success I have been getting in my investors' public seminars came directly from learning how to break through the negative connotations I had to public speaking. Your exercises in the video were powerful and effective."*
—John Harold, Financial Planner

**60-minute video**                                          **Order #V2, $37**

165

**172 pages, hard-cover book**

## Conquer Fear! Ending Procrastination and Self-Sabotage to Achieve What You Really Want

Why is it that two people can take the same goal-setting class, and one will achieve their goals, while the other will allow fear, lack of focus, procrastination and self-sabotage to destroy their efforts, and never accomplish the very thing they say they want? That very question, and experiencing it countless times with the sales force I was leading in a direct selling company, led me to write this book, *Conquer Fear*.

Most books written on this subject only cover the psychology factor of fear, which doesn't create lifelong change. There's something deeper. The other factor that, Conquer Fear answers is an issue of the heart. The way to conquer fear and create courage is to cultivate faith. The opposite of fear is faith. It is faith that fosters courage, boldness and conviction. It is only through faith that we can banish fear, anxiety, procrastination, and all the other symptoms that fear creates. The missing link was that most people don't cultivate their faith. They have negative belief barriers that limit their success. The startling truth is, "The only person keeping you from achieving your goals is you."

**Change your beliefs—and you change your behaviors.**

**Change your behaviors—and you change your results.**

It was when we began living our life by this statement that we began to see incredible success:

*Conquer Fear*, through the blending of the two disciplines of psychology and theology, is your tool to changing your results through first changing your beliefs. Through this book, you will discover the core truths about goal-setting, maintaining focus, motivation, and creating momentum. You will uncover the reasons behind why you do what you do. You will uncover the hidden needs and beliefs behind your behavior, and cultivate your faith so you have the courage to change them.

Whether you are an entrepreneur, a director of a company or a parent, Conquer Fear will empower you to break through procrastination. self-limiting beliefs, and cultivate your courage to accomplish all you're meant to achieve. —L. J.

**172 pages, hard-cover book**                    **Order #B2, $27**

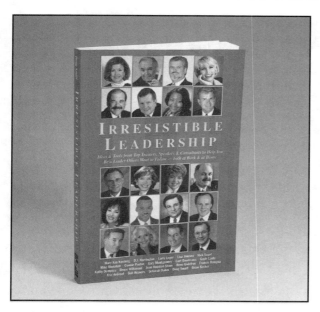

## Irresistible Leadership
## How to Be a Leader Others Will Follow

This just-released book is what you need to develop leadership skills to influence others and implement change. It's an anthology collection from twenty experts with successful strategies you can use to lead — at work and at home.

Chapters include:

Communication Tools for Tomorrow's Leaders;

A Simple Leadership Secret;

Leading from the Inside Out; and,

Secrets for Motivating Others to Do What You Want.

We know you'll especially love the chapter from Lisa Jimenez entitled, Leadership by Conviction — Raising Success to Significance. You'll learn the one essential quality that makes great leaders. You'll also learn how to convey your convictions in a way that empowers the people you lead. Lisa presents action steps that will help you identify any self-limiting beliefs keeping you from becoming the leader you are meant to be. So, make sure this book is in your business library.

**Order #B1, $20**

## Conquer Fear! on Audio CD

This album will change the way you do business and the way you live your life. You will finally break through bad habits and negative beliefs that have been holding you back. If you've read, *Conquer Fear*, then you'll love listening to its powerful message on tape, over and over again! If you want to multiply your income and begin enjoying a dimension of joy you might not even be able to imagine... listen to *Conquer Fear*! on this 5 audio CD set, read by the author.

**4 audio CDs**                                          **Order #A4, $47**

## Radical Recruiting! on 6 Audio CDs & Workbook

Learn how to attract and recruit the winners! This audio album should be in every Network Marketer's library. In it, you will learn how to change your mindset and shatter your fear of recruiting. You'll master the 5-step sponsoring process and learn how to create an easy to use follow-up system. You'll learn the secrets to crafting a powerful presentation and one-on-one talk. You have all you need to build the organization you've always dreamed of. Learn how to use it to your ultimate advantage with this powerful six audio CD album and workbook.

Radical Recruiting will help you build your organization fast. You will learn an easy to duplicate 5-step recruiting process that will help you:

- Discover and eliminate your hidden fears about prospecting;
- Find out where to find the best prospects;
- Learn how to make powerful presentations to build your image—and your confidence;
- Practice the best strategy for successful follow-up;
- Discover the secrets to overcome the toughest objections;
- Learn the most effective close to help your prospect say yes; and
- Create momentum to make building your business more fun.

If you're serious about enrolling more leaders, making more money, and having more fun prospecting, then Radical Recruiting can show you the way. In this program, Lisa Jimenez M.Ed., digs deep to the root of prospecting to show you how to take your business to the next level. Lisa will empower you with the personal growth tools and dynamite prospecting skills you need to boost your business now! She uses her real-world experience of building a big business herself, to show you how to attract and retain the winners. Lisa's 5-step recruiting process is motivating to follow and gets results.

**6 audio CDs and 32-page workbook**          **Order #A5, $127**

## 27 Tips to Radical Recruiting! E-Coaching Program

27 Tips delivered via email in your inbox each day for 27 days to motivate and inspire your radical recruiting efforts! These are the personal growth tools and dynamite prospecting skills you need to boost your business now!

Picture this... every morning, first thing when you get up, you open your e-mail and I'm in your inbox. I'm there with one specific thing you can do that day to grow your business just a little bit more. The next day, another e-mail bell—it's another message from me with another tip to help you find yet one more leader for your organization. Day three another bell... Day four another bell...

For the next 27 days you and I are going to be connected in a journey of challenge, adventure and growth. These recruiting tips will take you to the upper reaches of your company's compensation plan!

$27

## 27 Tips to Conquering Your Fear! E-Coaching

Online Coaching Program. 27 Tips delivered via email in your inbox each day for 27 days to help you Conquer Your Fears and Achieve Your Dreams!

$27

# Here's How To Order

Our staff is ready to answer your questions and assist you with your mail or phone order. Please use this order form to organize your phone order before you call our toll-free number. Order online www.Rx-Success.com.

Your Name _____

MLM Co. _____

Address _____

City _____ State _____ Zip _____

Office Phone _____ Home Phone _____

Fax _____

**PHONE:** **1-800-489-7391 or (954) 755-3670**

**FAX:** **(954) 796-0549**

**MAIL:** **Rx Success, Inc.**

**4630 N. University Dr. Suite #449**

**Coral Springs, FL 33067**

Method of Payment:

____ Check or Money Order payable to Rx Success, Inc.
No cash or CODs please.

____ Visa ____ M/C ____ Amex ____ Diners ____ Discover

Card Number _____

Expiration _____ Signature _____

For shipments to an address other than your own, fill in below:

Your Name _____

Address _____

City _____ State _____ Zip _____

Phone _____

Gift Card To _____

From _____

*90-day, 100% money back guarantee on
items returned in resalable condition.*